Transport and Society

Trains

G. Freeman Allen

Wayland

Transport and Society

Motor Cars
Submarines
Buses
Passenger Aircraft
Lorries, Vans and Trucks
Trains
Motorbikes
Merchant Ships

First published in 1982 by
Wayland Publishers Ltd
49 Lansdowne Place, Hove
East Sussex BN3 1HF, England

ISBN 0 85340 960 9

Phototypeset by
Kalligraphics Ltd, Redhill, Surrey
Printed in Italy by
G. Canale & C.S.p.A., Turin
Bound in the U.K. by
The Pitman Press, Bath

Contents

Why Railways were Born

Britain was the first country to perfect the steam railway. This was because the huge, sudden increase in industrial activity known as the Industrial Revolution started in Britain at the beginning of the nineteenth century.

New factory towns sprang up inland; demand for raw materials rose and so did the amount of finished goods to be carried to the coastal ports. The growing populations of the cities needed more food from the countryside too. All this created a need for a more efficient form of transport than the canal barges or horse-drawn wagons of the period.

That was the spur to Britain's steam railway pioneers. Other countries were inspired by Britain's example, and they built the railways first; in

One of the earliest forms of railway – a sixteenth-century miner pushes his cart along a track made from wooden planks.

The steam-powered road carriage was one of the first attempts to use steam for transport.

those countries it was the existence of railways which encouraged industrial development.

There were primitive railways long before the steam engine. As far back as the start of the sixteenth century, coal miners in Germany had found they could push heavier loads in their carts if their wheels ran on a smooth track. They made this crude track by laying parallel lines of wooden planks over the rough ground. The problem, of course, was to stop the carts' flat-rimmed wheels wandering off the 'track'. That was solved in the mid-eighteenth century by the invention of flanged wheels and iron rails. These were first tried on wagonways which used horses for power.

By the start of the nineteenth century steam power was being used to drive factory machines. Several inventors, such as James Watt and William Murdoch, had been trying to make a workable steam-powered road carriage, but it was the Cornish engineer Richard Trevithick who first realized that much more benefit could be got from steam if it was used to drive a locomotive on a wagonway. He was the first to build a usable steam locomotive, which successfully moved a train of 15 tonnes of iron at South Wales' Pen-y-Darren ironworks in 1804.

George Stephenson's engine Locomotion, *which hauled the first load on the Stockton & Darlington Railway.*

Trevithick got no further because the wagonway rails were not strong enough to carry his locomotive without breaking, and because the South Wales ironworkers were afraid jobs would be lost if their horses were replaced. But rails were soon made tougher, and, as the Industrial Revolution took off, there was more work and less need to worry about jobs.

However, it was the demand for the coal of North-East England which brought the steam locomotive to perfection. By 1820 William Hedley, Timothy Hackworth and George Stephenson had all devised locomotives that could haul quite heavy loads up the steep inclines of the north-eastern colliery wagonways for which they were the chief engineers.

But these were private railways – they carried only the collieries' goods. So far the only public railways, open to carry anyone's goods, had been horse-worked. Now the locomotive was capable enough to allow the planning of the first public steam railway, the Stockton & Darlington. Its promoters were local businessmen who desperately needed an easier way to move coal from the mines in South Durham to the harbour at Stockton on the River Tees.

Though his engineering was entirely self-taught,

George Stephenson so impressed the businessmen that they made him their engineer. Not only did he build the Stockton & Darlington Railway, but it was his engine, *Locomotion*, which triumphantly hauled a load of 69 tonnes over the 34 km (21 miles) from Shildon to Stockton on 27 September 1825 to open the line. But people still did not entirely trust the steam locomotive's reliability: for eight years the S&D's passengers were pulled by horses; only its goods were hauled by steam locomotives.

Straight away the new railway attracted good business because it was much cheaper to use than road carts, besides being more efficient, and it was soon making a great deal of money for its owners. News of this success encouraged the construction of the first railways in Continental Europe – in Austria in 1827 and France a year later – and in America, where the first stretch of the Baltimore & Ohio Railroad was opened in April 1827.

These earliest railways had been built primarily to carry goods. The first to be planned with both passengers and goods in mind was the Liverpool &

The opening of the Stockton & Darlington Railway, 27 September 1825.

A replica of Robert Stephenson's Rocket.

Manchester Railway. There were very good reasons for this: industrial development had more than doubled the population of each of the two cities since 1790 alone, and they were not very far apart in distance.

Again George Stephenson won the chief engineer's job. But now he could leave the locomotive side to his brilliant son, Robert, while he concentrated on the very difficult tracklaying, bridge-building and tunnelling side of the project. So Robert was mainly responsible for the success of *Rocket*, the engine which won the 1829 Rainhill Trails which the Liverpool & Manchester company held to find the best locomotive for their railway.

The L&MR's open day, 15 September 1830, was spoiled by a tragedy, when one of the important guests, the elderly politician William Huskisson, stumbled as he crossed the track in front of *Rocket* and was killed. But the public soon forgot that. Almost at once the railway was carrying twice as many passengers between Liverpool and Manchester as the road's stagecoaches had been doing before it opened. By the end of 1830, more than half of the stagecoach operators had been driven out of business.

Naturally, other cities hurried to start building railways. By 1851 you could travel by train from

London to Birmingham, Liverpool, Manchester, Bristol and Southampton, and Scotland had its first railways. In that year the number of rail-passenger journeys was already over 80 million. On the roads alongside the new railways, the stagecoaches had almost disappeared.

The new trains were not only faster: more importantly, they were vastly cheaper to ride in. Working families could now afford pleasure trips they could never have considered by stagecoach. Without railways the Great Exhibition of British goods, put on in London's spectacular Crystal Palace in 1851, would not have drawn six million visitors. The total was so high only because many thousands of families were attracted to travel to London from the provinces by trains charging one-tenth of the stagecoach fare, or even less. Furthermore, only trains could have moved people in such huge numbers.

The passenger train also helped to speed up industrial growth. Factories could find extra workers more easily because countryfolk were more ready to take a job in the towns, knowing how easily and cheaply they could return to their families at the

Passenger and goods trains on the Liverpool & Manchester Railway, 1831. The train at the top of the picture is for first-class passengers, and the one below it is for second and third class.

weekend. In time many of their families joined them in industrial towns, so that the railway was also responsible for taking people away from many market towns in the country.

Many of the popular seaside resorts owe their size to the townsfolk who began to flood in after railways had been built. In one summer week of 1859, for example, the number of people travelling by train to the south-coast resort of Brighton was bigger than the town's population. At that time Brighton was growing ten times as fast as the country's most prosperous industrial city, Bradford.

Canal owners (in America as much as in Europe) fought much harder than the stagecoach operators to stop the spread of railways. But although some canals were forced to close in the mid-nineteenth century, many continued to make a good living. Barges were unreliable and terribly slow, but for carriage of goods that were not urgent they were considerably cheaper than the trains.

As the nineteenth century moved into its second half, Scandinavia was the only area of Europe still without its first railway. Many Continental railways started work with British-built locomotives,

A mid-nineteenth-century poster designed to encourage people to travel by train to the seaside.

A westbound train in the USA, 1868.

particularly of the Stephenson design. A number of them were also built with the help of British workmen or 'navvies' – a nickname which was short for 'inland navigators', as the men who had dug British canals were called – and under the management of British railway-building contractors.

The first railway planners in America had the hardest job of all to break down opposition to the new form of transport. It came not only from people making money out of roads and canals, but also from clergymen, who really believed that the steam engine was an invention of the devil.

So far only the eastern side of the USA had been developed. The people were eager to drive westward, but the mountain ranges fringing the eastern territory stood in the way. As soon as it became clear that railways could carry goods through those mountains much more easily than canals, businessmen and traders were less ready to listen to the opponents of railways.

Railway-building quickly spread right the way down the eastern side of the USA, from the Canadian border to the Gulf of Mexico, and by 1850 the Americans were putting down more new track per year than the rest of the world put together.

The Railway Becomes Big Business

By the mid-nineteenth century the fast-spreading railways of Europe and America had already become the chief means of moving passengers and goods in bulk. It was clear that the way they developed would have a very powerful influence on each country's future – where its industry would be concentrated; how its raw materials could be exploited; and, not least, where and how its people would live. Railways could well have vital military value as well.

This faced governments with a key question: should the planning and operation of something so important to the future industrial and daily life of

Early European railways – the first train to run between Leipzig and Berlin in Germany, and a view of Leipzig station.

The British 'railway mania' of 1845–47: businessmen rush to present their plans for new railways.

their people be left entirely to private business? If railways were built only where businessmen thought they could make a lot of money, the result could easily be wasteful competition in the rich industrial areas and neglect of the countryside.

On the continent of Europe every government soon decided to take at least some control of the new form of transport, and this had two very important consequences. First, it set the stage for the total state takeover of railways, which one country after another ordered in the next century, when some private companies were in danger of financial disaster because of new motor-transport competition.

Second, the countries of Continental Europe came to accept that railways needed the support of government money just as much as roads or canals. Their people came to expect trains to be provided as a national service, like the post or the police, and they took it for granted that at least some of the cost of running railways would be met by the government out of general taxation.

That explains why, nowadays, the countries of

George Hudson, the 'Railway King', who fraudulently won control of more than 2,000 km (1,250 miles) of British railway. His frauds were discovered, however, and he fled the country in 1855.

Continental Europe are prepared to spend so much more – in proportion to their population – to provide a convenient, modern rail service than Britain. It was not until the passage of its 1968 Transport Act that Britain first decided to give its railways a sum of public money every year, to help cover the costs of running passenger trains and thus keep the price of using them reasonable.

Both in Britain and America, although government permission was needed to build a railway, the planning and running of railways was left entirely in private business. Britain's first railways quickly made so much profit that businessmen all over the country rushed to jump on the bandwagon. From 1845 to 1847 the nation was gripped by a 'railway mania' – so much so that in 1846 alone Parliament was asked to approve proposals for no fewer than

Railways were even bigger business in the USA than in Britain, and Cornelius Vanderbilt was one of the best-known American 'Railway Barons'.

815 different new railways! Even though many of these schemes were pipe dreams, there were enough sound plans to have a quarter of a million men employed on British railway-building by the end of the 1840s. At that point, as much as one-tenth of the country's national wealth was being invested in railway-building.

Fierce and often unscrupulous competition was the natural result. The rich industrial areas of the country were plastered with rival lines. Thus Manchester, for example, eventually had four different companies fighting for its traffic from London; and Carlisle's goods traffic was shunted into and out of nine different yards.

This boom soon bred its empire-builders, some of whom would not merely cheat in their financial dealings to get more railways under their control, but would even organize violence to stop rival railways breaking into territory they considered their own. The most famous of the British railway rogues was George Hudson, the so-called 'Railway King'. Starting life as a draper in York, by 1848 this cunning man had won control of more than a quarter of the 8,000 km (5,000 miles) of British railway then open for business. But the frauds by which he had won that control became known. Every railway of which he was chairman threw him out and he fled the country in 1855.

On 10 May 1869 a golden spike was driven in to mark the completion of the Union Pacific – the first railway running from one side of the USA to the other.

The northern end of the St Gotthard Tunnel in Switzerland, which was opened in 1886.

In America, where railways became even bigger business, the likes of Hudson were known as the 'Railway Barons'. One of the best-known was Cornelius Vanderbilt, the head of the New York Central, whose trains were roaming as much as 16,000 km (10,000 miles) of railway route by the end of the nineteenth century. One famous saying of his not only indicates the attitude of so many of the British and American railway-builders in the last century, but also shows how railways were dominating the world of industry. 'Law!', Vanderbilt shouted in the course of an argument, 'What do I care about law? Ain't I got the power?'

By the close of the nineteenth century, the last big gaps in the Western world's railway systems had been closed. Starting with the Union Pacific's completion in May 1869, the Americans had finished five routes crossing the whole country. Canada's first transcontinental railway, the Canadian Pacific, was opened in 1866. In Europe the Alpine barrier had been conquered by the first of the continent's great tunnels – the Semmering in Austria, with which a direct route from Austria and Hungary was opened up in 1853. Next came the Mont Cenis tunnel, between Italy and France, in 1871; and then the first of Switzerland's, the St Gotthard, built in 1886.

The Railway Heyday

During the first fifty years of railways, train travel was pretty uncomfortable unless you could afford to ride first-class. Most third-class travellers in Britain rode in open wagons until 1844, when Parliament passed a law which compelled the railways to run, on each of their routes, at least one train a day that gave third-class passengers both a place to sit and protection from the weather. However, many more years were to pass before third-class passengers were admitted to the fastest express trains.

As late as the 1860s few trains either in Europe or America had lavatories. Passengers had to wait until the train reached a station, which was also the only place where they could eat on a train journey.

Third-class passengers on their way to Brighton, on the south coast of England, in 1859.

A·Pullman dining and bar car.

The third-class seats were of plain wood; even in second class the wood was only very thinly covered with material. The sole form of heating was a coal or wood stove; the lighting confined to a foul-smelling oil lamp.

The discomforts of the early trains were naturally felt most on the long rail routes of America and Continental Europe, where many passengers travelled overnight. And it was an American, George Pullman, who inspired the great improvement in train comfort which began in the last quarter of the nineteenth century.

In 1864–65 Pullman persuaded a few American railroads that travellers would be prepared to pay extra for proper beds on overnight trains. Pullman himself built the sleeping cars, the first of which were 'convertible' – that is, they had day-travel seats which could be turned into beds at night. The railroads ran the cars in their trains and pocketed the passengers's basic fares: Pullman made his living from the additional fees the passengers had to

pay for using his cars and their services.

Soon Pullman hit on the idea of putting a small kitchen at one end of the car to serve his customers with meals in their berths. From that it was a short step to the construction of the first Pullman dining car, in 1868. By the end of the century America's Pullman-equipped trains were literally hotels on wheels. But they were for the customers with money; the non-Pullman American train passenger still travelled in much less comfort – and his trains were slower too.

The picture was similar in Continental Europe. There, Pullman's triumph had prompted a young Belgian, Georges Nagelmackers, to start an international sleeping-car service on the same pattern in 1873. His company also moved into restaurant cars in 1880 (though Europe's first restaurant car service had been pioneered by the British Great Northern Railway between London and Leeds a year earlier). As the century ended, the luxury trains of Nagelmackers' Wagon-Lits company were criss-crossing Europe. But they were the trains

European railways soon caught on to Pullman's idea of sleeping cars and restaurant cars for their wealthier passengers. This picture, taken in 1905, shows a restaurant car in Baghdad, Iraq.

of princes, ambassadors and bankers, and were too expensive for ordinary folk.

It was Britain's Midland Railway which sparked off the great improvement of rail travel for the general public (though it was also the Midland which introduced Pullmans to Britain, in 1875). The Midland was the last to complete a through route from London to Scotland. To win traffic from the earlier East and West Coast routes, it therefore decided, in 1875, to accept third-class travellers on all its trains, even the fastest; and at the same time it built much more comfortable coaches for second- and third-class travellers.

The Midland's enterprise not only forced its rivals to follow suit: it also drove them to a fierce competition in speed, which made other railways in Europe and America realize how much more passenger business they might attract if their trains went faster.

In 1888 and again in 1895, the whole British public was fascinated by real 'Races to the North', when for a few summer weeks the East and West Coast companies each deliberately sent their overnight trains away from London at the same time, and set out to reach Scotland ahead of the rival. In the 1895 race, the winning West Coast train reached Aberdeen in an unbelievable three hours less than the timetable of the period normally allowed. It was now clear that express trains could be run safely at 120 km/h (75 mph) or even more, and the other railways of Europe and, particularly, America were quick to respond to the British speed

During the last quarter of the nineteenth century, railways came to realize that they could attract more passengers if their trains were faster and more comfortable.

challenge.

Most of the world's great railway stations were built in the late nineteenth and early twentieth centuries. At first goods and passengers had been dealt with in the same place, but from about 1850 the railways began to build separate stations. As traffic grew, hotels, dining rooms and offices were made

American railways were quick to respond to the British speed challenge: this train averaged 96 km/h (60 mph) for much of the distance between New York and Chicago.

part of many big city passenger stations. And as the railway became one of the most important influences on business and everyday life, railways naturally set out to make the main station buildings at least as elegant and striking as any others in each city. The climax came in 1912 with the completion of New York's two-level Grand Central station, with a combined total of sixty-nine tracks serving forty-six platforms.

Although Henry Ford had produced the first popular motor car, his famous Model T, in 1908, it was not until 1913 that he developed a cheap method of manufacture – the assembly-line process – which drastically reduced the price of motor vehicles. Then, after the First World War (1914–18), long-distance buses came into general use. By the end of the 1920s, American people were travelling five times as far by car as by train, and European railways were starting to lose passengers too.

The people who were deserting the trains were not the users of the expensive luxury trains but the general public, who had so far benefited least from the railways' speed-up and comfort improvements. At last the railways of both America and Europe woke up to the needs of passengers they had taken too much for granted.

The early years of the twentieth century saw the building of many large, elegant railway stations.

During the 1930s, many previously all-Pullman trains in America had ordinary coaches added to them – and in most cases coaches of a much higher standard than before. Most of Britain's railways were now a little more concerned with raising the general standard of their express-train speed and comfort than to pay special attention to a handful of prestige trains.

But the railways could not stop the loss of some of their business to the roads. The shut down of country branch lines began before the Second World War because cars, buses and lorries were so much cheaper for local journeys and could deliver straight to the doorstep. Lorries were also robbing railways of some of their longer-distance freight – the goods which it was easiest to transport and which brought the highest revenue, such as food and household equipment.

The shutdown of British country lines began before the Second World War, as railways lost business to the roads.

The development of the diesel locomotive led to a great increase in train speed. This picture shows an early American diesel, the Flying Yankee.

Early in the 1930s, even the railways' first-class passenger business was threatened by the coming of the first airline services in Germany and America. This drove the railways to a remarkable speed-up of their principal express trains in the last few years before the Second World War broke out in September 1939. This was the age of the streamlined train, the years when 160 km/h (100 mph) first became a daily routine on a few important inter-city routes in Germany, America and Britain.

But though steam locomotives still pulled a few of the American and European high-speed trains (and all Britain's streamliners were steam-hauled), the great American speed-up, in particular, was only possible because of a new form of railway power – the diesel.

From Steam to Diesel and Electric Power

For their first hundred years, the world's railways were ruled by steam power. During that time locomotives grew steadily bigger and more powerful to meet the rising demand for goods transport and passenger-train speed and comfort. The higher standards of passenger comfort affected the need for more power because making passenger coaches more comfortable also made them heavier, without increasing the number of people they carried.

But although the great steam locomotives of the twentieth century looked so different from Robert Stephenson's *Rocket*, no one had found a better way to power a locomotive than to raise steam in a fire-tube boiler, and then use it in cylinders to drive pistons which imparted motion to road wheels

A section through a steam locomotive. The heat of the furnace causes water in the boiler to turn to steam, and the pressure of this steam forces the pistons to move and turn the road wheels.

One of the largest steam locomotives ever built – a Union Pacific 'Big Boy'.

through rods. Greater power became possible because the availability of stronger materials, such a steel, allowed engineers to build bigger boilers of higher steam pressure. Engineers learned, too, how to make steam flow more freely from boiler to cylinders, and from cylinders to exhaust, which was important in an engine designed to go fast. Track was also made steadily stronger, to withstand the increasing weight of locomotives.

The biggest steam locomotives were the monsters built to haul goods trains of up to 10,000 tonnes weight up the steep gradients of American railroads, especially the long climbs which carried the transcontinental routes over the mountain ranges inland from the west coast. These giants were 'articulated': that is, one enormous boiler fed two separate sets of cylinders and powered wheels.

The most massive of them were the so-called 'Big Boys' of the Union Pacific Railroad, which were almost 40.5 m (133 ft) long. A 'Big Boy' locomotive alone weighed 345 tonnes, but to supply its great boiler it also needed a tender weighing as much as 195 tonnes.

By the late 1930s, several American and European railways had steam locomotives capable of running express trains day in and day out at 160 km/h (100 mph) or even more, where main

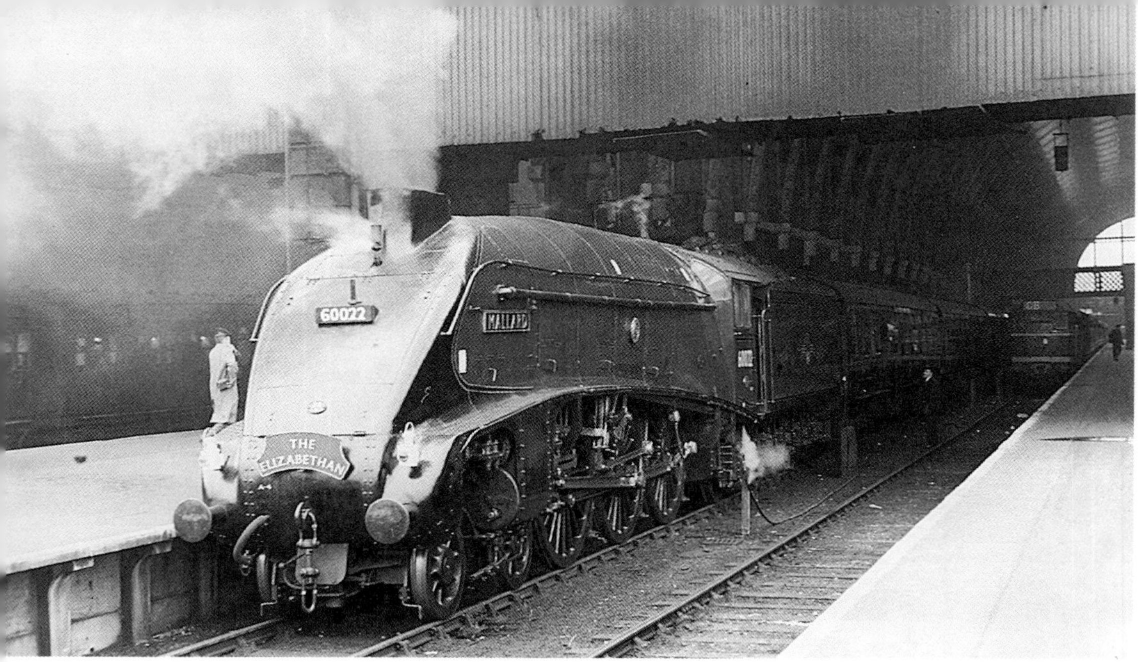

Mallard, *the locomotive which, in July 1938, reached 203 km/h (124½ mph) – a world record for steam.*

lines were reasonably free of curves and steep gradients. Between Chicago and Minneapolis, for example, the Milwaukee company of America had streamlined locomotives which could run its nine-coach 'Hiawatha' comfortably at an average speed of 145 km/h (90 mph) for hours on end.

In 1935, the German Reichsbahn built a streamlined locomotive which reached 200 km/h (124½ mph). That was the world record for steam until July 1938, when *Mallard*, one of the streamliners produced for the 1935–39 high-speed expresses of Britain's London North Eastern Railway, was whipped up to 203 km/h (126 mph) on a test run.

Mallard's feat was never beaten because by 1938 other forms of power were already threatening the rule of steam. The electric railway had been born, first in the form of low-powered city tramways, before the end of the nineteenth century. The first main-line electrification came in 1906, on the Swiss route across the Alps and through the Simplon Tunnel to Italy. But although that quickly proved the superiority of an electric locomotive in starting and hauling loads uphill, railways did not rush to electrify.

There were two reasons for this slow start. One was the fact that it took many years to find a satisfactory means of converting the high-voltage current of the national supply system into current suitable for a locomotive's motors. For this job, early electric locomotives had to carry machinery which was far too bulky and heavy.

The second reason was that an electric locomotive could not work unless live rails were laid or wires put up to supply it with power. That was a very expensive business, which had to be paid for before any electric trains could run.

So, to make electrification worthwhile, a railway had to be very busy – like a city underground or suburban line, for instance – or there had to be some other special reasons. In Switzerland, for example, the railway system was almost entirely electrified before the Second World War, not only because electric locomotives were so much more efficient on the steep Alpine gradients, but also because the country was so rich in rushing mountain rivers. Their strength could be used to drive turbines and generate electricity very cheaply. Furthermore, Switzerland, like Austria and Italy, had no coal mines of its own. After the First World

An American electric locomotive of the early 1930s.

War, coal became rather scarce in Europe; and more power could be got from a tonne of coal by burning it in an electric generating station than in a locomotive boiler. This was the first black mark against the steam locomotive as more efficient types of railway power came on to the scene.

The second was that it could not be run for much more than eight hours continuously without needing time off for clearance of soot and ash, let alone taking on fresh supplies of coal and water. An electric locomotive could run for at least a week on end without any attention.

So apart from the electric locomotive's superiority in acceleration and load-pulling, its continuous readiness for work meant that an electric train service could be run with fewer locomotives and fewer locomotive men than under steam. This would become a very important difference after the Second World War, when wages rose rapidly and railways were very anxious to cut the number of their workers. Then, too, it became more and more difficult to find men willing to work in the unavoidably filthy conditions of steam locomotive cabs and servicing sheds.

But as has already been said, it cost a great deal of money to change to electric power. Had it not been for the perfection of the diesel locomotive, steam might have lasted longer.

Steam locomotive servicing sheds were unavoidably filthy, and it became increasingly difficult to get men to work in such conditions.

Diesel-electric engines being overhauled in one of British Rail's workshops.

With a diesel engine one could build an electric locomotive that produced its own current and did not need to be supplied from wires or a live rail. The diesel engine did not drive the wheels directly. It powered a generator producing electric current, which was then fed to electric motors that moved the locomotive. Although many low-powered locomotives and railcars have been and still are built in which diesel engines drive the road wheels through gears, as in lorries, there is a limit to the power which can be passed through gears without submitting them to too much strain. Almost all main-line locomotives are moving 'power stations' (diesel-electrics) of the kind first described.

For a number of reasons, it is impossible to pack as much power or such rapid acceleration into a diesel-electric as into a 'straight' electric locomotive of the same size. A diesel-electric also needs more day-to-day servicing, though nothing like as much as a steam engine.

Throughout the 1930s, diesel engines became more and more powerful. They climbed the hills with heavy loads so much better than steam, could get streamliners up to high speed so much more quickly, and were so much cheaper to run, that the

Throughout the 1940s and 1950s, many American steam locomotives were scrapped and replaced by diesels like this.

American railroads hurried to get rid of their steam power. In the twenty years up to 1960, over 40,000 American steam locomotives were scrapped and replaced by fewer diesels.

But oil was not as cheap in Europe as in America. Besides, after the Second World War, the French found a way to use high-voltage current straight from the national grid for railway electrification. This not only reduced the cost of electrification, but made it possible to get still more power for each tonne of locomotive weight. The extraordinarily rapid advance of electronics has since achieved more improvements, both in the power obtained per tonne and also in locomotive efficiency. It is now possible to build an extremely powerful electric locomotive weighing only 80 tonnes, which is just as much at home hauling 200-km/h (125-mph) passenger trains as on heavy coal-carrying trains.

After the Second World War, therefore, most European railways were turning to diesel power solely as a stop-gap until they could electrify all their main routes. But when the Arab–Israeli war of 1973 was followed by a dramatic increase in the price of oil – and the realization that supplies of oil would be exhausted early in the next century – country after country decided to increase the pace of its electrification of railways, whatever the cost.

Railways Change the Cities

Right from the start of the Industrial Revolution, people with money – factory owners, merchants, lawyers and the like – had been moving house from the smoky town and city centres to the nearby countryside. They could afford their own horse-drawn carriages to get them to and from their places of work, or to commute, as we say nowadays.

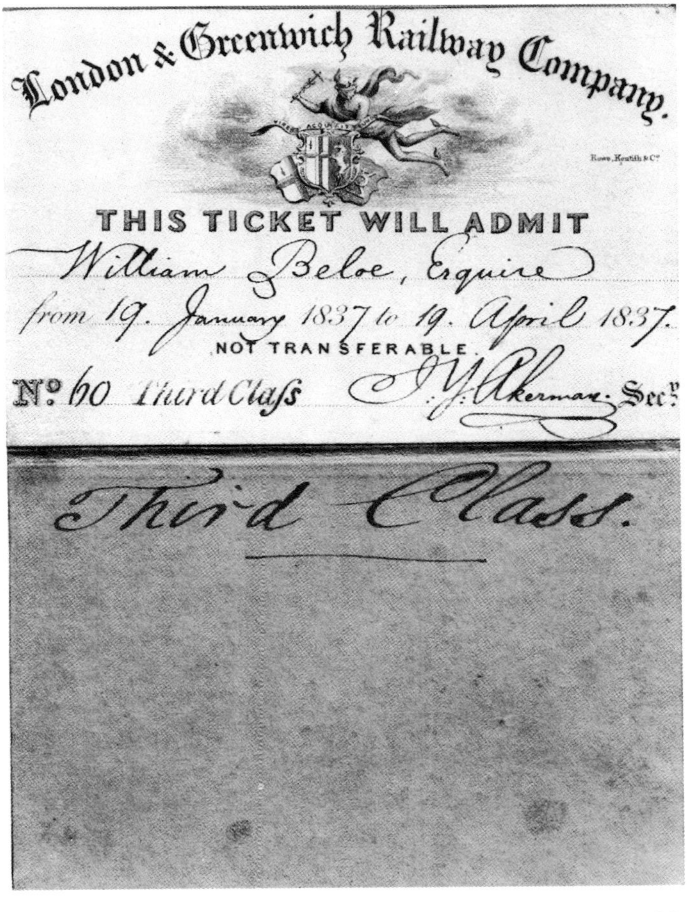

One of the first railway season tickets ever issued. In the second half of the nineteeth century, more and more short, local lines were built and commuting became cheap enough for everyone.

In the second half of the nineteenth century, when the railways had completed their main routes and could turn to building short, local lines, commuting became cheap enough for everyone.

The result, naturally, was a rapid spread of housing and population from the towns and cities to the suburbs. But though city workers were living over a wider area, they were still massing in the city centre for their jobs every day. By the end of the century

In its early days, the New York Elevated Railway was worked by steam.

High above the road, a New York 'El' train takes a curve. Electric trains were first used in New York just before the end of the nineteenth century.

most of the world's cities were suffering appalling congestion in their streets. This prompted construction of railways through city centres, with stations very closely spaced so that they would be as convenient for short journeys as the horse-drawn buses and tramways in the streets.

Railways of this kind are generally known as Metropolitan (Metro for short) or, more recently, as Urban Rapid Transit. In some cities, the first of them were built above ground, and mostly on viaducts above streets to save finding room for them on the surface. This gained them the name of Elevated Railways, or, in America, 'Els'. The most famous, in New York and Chicago, were both worked by steam at the start. At the beginning of this century the New York 'El' operated thirty-six routes, totalling 450 km (280 miles) of track, and was used for a staggering total of 250 million journeys a year.

London was the first city to build a Metro underground, from Paddington to Farringdon Street. This began operation in January 1863, also with steam power, which made a journey through the tunnels a choking experience. Fortunately, as we have already seen, the electric railway was perfected before the end of the nineteenth century. Some cities, such as Paris in 1900, ran their Metros

For the first quarter of this century, many of the world's major cities built new Metro systems. Besides taking people into the cities to work and to the shops, Metros also enabled people to spend their leisure time in the countryside around the cities.

electrically from the start; a few years earlier Chicago and New York had begun the change to electricity (New York also started to change from 'El' to underground railways in 1900); and in 1903 London's Metro abandoned steam for electric power.

For the first quarter of this century, the world's cities busily built new Metros and the railways steadily electrified their city suburban lines. In the last few years before the Second World War, however, the pace slowed. Family cars had become so much cheaper and were in such wide use, and buses had become so much more efficient that town-dwellers were less keen to use local railways.

Since 1950, there has been a dramatic increase in the building of new Metros throughout the world. This picture was taken during the construction of the Eastern Suburbs Railway in Sydney, Australia.

Immediately after the war, private car ownership increased so rapidly that many cities, particularly in the USA, felt at first that it was more important to build new city-centre roads and car parks than to spend money on railways.

Since about 1950 there has been a dramatic change. In the past thirty years, six times as many new Metros have been opened as between 1907 and 1935; and in 1982, with seventy-one world cities already operating Metros and many of them planning extensions, sixteen more had started to build their first Metro. Why?

Long before the oil price explosion of 1973, which made the public more wary of using their cars, cities in the USA, as well as in Europe, decided that if they went on knocking down buildings to make room for new roads and car parks, they would eventually destroy the quality of city life. They realized, too, that there would never come a time when road systems were big enough. As soon as a new road was built, it attracted more cars, which created traffic jams that needed new roads elsewhere, which in turn became overcrowded, calling for more new roads – and so on.

This process can be halted by introducing what we call an 'integrated public transport system', as has been done in the big cities of West Germany, like Frankfurt, Munich, Hamburg and Stuttgart. Most bus routes do not compete with railways, but make rounds of the suburbs to collect commuters and deliver them to rail stations. These suburban stations are also well provided with car parks so that people can drive themselves to the train if they prefer. The suburban railway then does the job at which it is best – carrying large numbers of people quickly and cheaply to the city centre.

But it no longer drops them inconveniently at terminal stations away from the city centre. The suburban railway has been extended in tunnels through the city's heart. In this underground cros-

French Metro trains at a station outside Paris.

The world's first unmanned Metro train, at Lille, in France.

sing of the city, it halts at handsome new stations where passengers can easily change to Metro lines that will take them on to their offices or to the shopping centre. The whole journey, by bus, suburban train and Metro, can be made on one inclusive ticket.

Governments and city authorities have also been encouraged to build new Metros because the age of the computer and microprocessor has made them the most labour-saving way of moving large numbers of people. The Metro is the easiest kind of railway to make fully automatic, because its route is simple, with very few junctions, and its trains are all the same. And electronics have made it comparatively easy to operate by remote control every piece of equipment on a train, as well as the points and signals along its route. Drivers are no longer necessary. However, as yet only one city, Lille, in France, has been bold enough to ask its people to ride in Metro trains which carry no driver, guard, or any other staff.

So the trains of a whole Metro system can be controlled from central computers working to timetables stored in their memory banks. Furthermore, ticket-issuing, change-giving and ticket-checking at platform turnstiles can now be done automatically, and stations can be supervised from a central control room by closed-circuit TV, so there is no need for station staff either.

The Greatest Challenge

The first problem facing the big railways of Western Europe after the Second World War was appalling damage. France, for example, found that shelling, bombing, sabotage and destruction by the retreating German armies had left more than three-quarters of her locomotives and over half of her railway system unusable.

With the help of American money loans and manufacturing, rebuilding was extraordinarily rapid. Because there was so much to reconstruct, it was also a golden opportunity to modernize. Together with another post-war shortage of coal, that was why most of the Continental European railways took the chance to begin extensive electrification, or else to buy diesels until they could electrify,

After the Second World War, many locomotives in Western Europe were found to be damaged beyond repair.

In 1948, the private railway companies in Britain were made into one State-owned system – British Railways. This train is painted in the early BR colours.

instead of replacing all their lost steam engines with the same number of new ones.

Britain's railways, on the other hand, were not severely damaged, only worn out by the work they had done and lack of proper upkeep during the war. So the Government put them at the end of the industrial queue for modernization. For the first ten post-war years, they had to be content with patching up wartime wear and tear. That was why Britain was much later than its neighbours in starting post-war main-line electrification.

By the time British Railways – the private companies were made one State-owned system by the Labour Government in 1948 – were at last allowed the means to modernize in 1955, the Western world's railways were facing a far more serious challenge from the road than any they had known in the 1930s. Driven by the demands of war, industry had developed a great deal of new technology in vehicle and engine design, and equally rapid and therefore cheaper mass production. New cars, and lorries which were more efficient than before the war, flooded on to the roads.

Road transport made a rapid advance in the West not only because it became more convenient and efficient from year to year, but because that meant it became cheaper to use too. The railways, on the other hand, could not reduce their costs anything like so easily.

Although the road user was taxed, what he paid

During the 1950s, trains on most British country lines were carrying fewer and fewer passengers and goods; buses, cars and lorries were cheaper and more convenient for local transport.

In the mid-1960s, many British country lines were closed in an attempt to save money.

did not cover the full cost of his roads and the police that controlled them. Many railways (but not Britain's or America's) received some government money to help pay for the upkeep of their track. But they had to meet the cost of all the complicated signalling and of the backroom and ground staff needed to plan and run their strictly-timetabled services, as well as the train crews themselves. In other words, more men and their wages were involved in running a train than a road vehicle. And in the post-war industrial boom, when it was workers not jobs which were scarce, wages were rising rapidly.

Obviously, then, every train needed to carry as many passengers or as much goods as possible to pay its way – and to carry them as far as possible. But on most country lines, trains were carrying less and less and thus costing more and more, because it was so much more convenient, and cheaper, to use a bus, car or lorry to deliver passengers and goods right to the doorstep.

The effect was most serious in Britain, because she was the only country in Western Europe which had always expected her railways to pay their way without government money. That was still the hope, even when they became state-owned; but by 1960 it was clear that this was impossible without drastic change.

Because of the huge size of the USA and Canada, lorries are unable to compete successfully with trains for goods movement.

In 1962 the British Government appointed an industrialist, Dr Richard Beeching, to head British Railways and plan the necessary changes. The result was that between 1963 and 1968 BR suffered huge cuts in the numbers of their lines, passenger stations, goods depots, rolling stock and staff. But Beeching still could not make BR pay. In its 1968 Transport Act, Britain at last had to accept that railways needed the pre-planned annual support of government money, rather than making good the losses after they had occurred.

Other European countries closed far fewer country lines. In one or two cases their governments would have liked to close considerably more – in Sweden and West Germany, for instance. But there the tradition of railways as a public service, irrespective of the public cost, was much stronger, as we have seen earlier. Consequently political and local opposition to closures was much more powerful and successful. So, today, France contentedly pays more than twice as much as Britain, and West Germany four times as much, out of national and local taxes to support railways.

We must not forget the additional impact of air competition. After the war, this developed most

In 1971, the US government provided money for a national railway corporation, Amtrak, designed to maintain a basic service of passenger trains on the main inter-city routes.

quickly and had the biggest effect in North America. Although the huge size of the USA and Canada limited the effect of road transport on goods movement, the longer the distance to be travelled, the easier it was for airlines to beat passenger trains hands down for speed.

With the added affect of road competition on shorter-distance passenger trains, the railroads not only began to cut their services, but, before long, to stop all passenger operation in many cases.

At that point many Americans took fright at the prospect of skies getting more and more dangerously crowded with aircraft, and of total reliance on the road for shorter journeys. In 1971 the Government put up the money for a national corporation, called Amtrak, to keep a basic service of passenger trains going over the country's key inter-city routes. In 1978 Canada did the same; there the passenger train operators are called Via Rail.

2631
2631

The Fight for Freight

The majority of the world's principal railways earn more from freight than from passengers. Britain has only joined the exceptions since the 1960s – an indication of how much goods traffic BR has lost to the roads since the last war. Its chief companions are other comparatively small countries where cities are close together, a good road system has been developed, and a great deal of goods move only short distances, so that lorries compete very keenly. Holland is one example, Japan another, though Japan's railways have also suffered because so much of the country's industry is on the coast and its great post-war industrial boom has exhausted local coal and minerals; they now come from abroad straight to the factories by sea, while small coastal ships are as sharp a competitor as lorries for other goods movement.

Since freight is so important financially, most railways have been just as concerned, if not more so, to find cheaper and more efficient ways of moving goods as to keep a grip on their passengers. It is not just a case of trying to stop lorries taking away from the trains goods they can easily carry, like food, household goods, TV sets and so on. Coal, for instance, can now be moved by pipeline just as well as oil. Also, in many countries with wide rivers or canals, huge barges, often coupled in 'trains', are now very competitive for movement of coal and minerals like ore, because they pay scarcely anything for the use of their 'track' – the water – even if it is a canal.

The railway's answer has to be to move more tonnage per train, with bigger wagons so that fewer

Today, the majority of the world's principal railways earn more money for freight than from passengers.

are needed, and to get more loaded runs out of each train per year. In this way the tonnage will also be shifted with fewer staff, saving yet more money. The railway will, as we say nowadays, be getting more productivity both from its hardware and from its manpower.

This was how British Rail sharply reduced the cost of moving coal by rail, so that coal was chosen as the fuel for many of Britain's big new power stations which were built in the 1960s, well before the shocking rise of oil prices after the Arab–Israeli War of 1973. BR did it by thinking up a scheme called 'Merry-Go-Round' which kept trains of new, high-capacity wagons travelling in an almost continuous circuit between the coalfields and the power stations. 'Merry-Go-Round' was based on what is called 'unit train' or 'block train' working, in which a goods train carries a full load from starting-point to destination and is not stopped on the way for expensive shunting in marshalling yards.

In BR's 'Merry-Go-Round' scheme even the locomotives stay coupled to their trains at the destination. At a power station the railway is laid out in a loop, in the middle of which the rails straddle huge coal bunkers. When a loaded train comes to these bunkers, the driver reduces the locomotive to a

A British Railways 'Merry-Go-Round' unit train leaves a colliery with a full load of coal for a power station.

In some continents, very long unit trains can be used to haul huge quantities of raw materials over great distances. This train is in Western Australia.

very low speed, and the train is unloaded without stopping. One by one the wagons have their floor doors opened by automatic devices, then closed the same way after their coal has been dropped between the rails into the bunkers below. And then the train completes the loop and heads straight back to the pits for a fresh load.

The unit train idea serves just as well where other industries depend on a big inflow of a certain raw material. The steel industry, for example, has to be fed with iron ore. Today few steelworks are close to sources of ore. Most of Europe's take their ore from Africa, Australia or South America, so that they need an efficient means of carrying it from a port to their works. One big West German steelworks near Hanover has all its ore unloaded at Hamburg, 225 km (140 miles) away, and brought to its doorstep in four daily unit trains of massive twelve-wheeled wagons; each train weighs 5,400 tonnes and carries 4,000 tonnes of ore.

In other continents, where railways are not so busy with passenger trains as they are in Europe, and where track and signalling arrangements allow very long trains to be run, the huge tonnage which modern diesel or electric locomotives can haul makes the unit train an economically viable way of moving raw materials very long distances.

But what use is the unit train in the huge goods market where the final delivery is to a factory, a shop or a private house that has no railway up to its doorstep, and when the goods to be delivered may not even fill one wagon, let alone a train? This is the valuable business which lorries have so largely snatched from the railways since the last war. But the railways desperately need to get more of it back; without it they do not have enough traffic of other kinds to cover all the special costs of running a railway.

Even here the unit train can do part of the job at an attractive price. Take the petrol for your family car. It will be delivered to your local garage by tanker lorry, but that tanker lorry will have filled up at a depot quite nearby, not at the coastal refinery where the oil was landed from the sea and turned into petrol. Many inland depots are supplied from the refinery by pipeline, but in a good many other cases it has been found that, rather than build an expensive pipeline, it is cheaper to use the existing railway and feed them with unit trains of 100-tonne tank wagons.

The unit train is certainly a much cheaper method than using a fleet of lorries to carry the same load from the coast – and moreover it helps to prevent road congestion and wear. In many countries politicians and public are now increasingly anxious to see more use of the railways, so as to control the nuisance and pollution of increased road traffic.

So here we have a marriage of rail and road – the railway carrying the goods as far as they can travel in bulk, and the lorry doing the final distribution in small lots. Each is doing the part of the job for which it is cheapest and best suited. And because of this, the goods are being moved with the least possible consumption of fuel. This is a consideration which means more and more to governments, as well as

It is cheaper to transport petrol from a refinery to inland depots by unit train than to build a new pipeline.

A trainload of containers is taken inland from the port of Wellington, New Zealand. Local distribution will be carried out by lorries.

manufacturers and customers, now that oil is not only very expensive, but certain to get scarcer.

In the past twenty years, the movement of manufacturered goods world-wide has been revolutionized by a simple invention that has made this worthwhile marriage of different forms of transport – what is known as 'inter-modal' transport – much easier. It is the container, which is the equivalent of a movable lorry body. Containers are mostly boxes with loading doors, but they can be tanks to carry liquids, or flat platforms for goods like steel bars. Their advantage is that they enable valuable goods to be carried from factory to user without any unloading or reloading on the way, even when the journey involves ships as well as land transport.

The greater part of the world's trade in manufactured goods is now carried out in containers, and railways have won a very large share of the movement of containers between ports and inland depots. Here again the movement of containers is so considerable that they can make up economical

Lorry trailers are loaded on to a piggyback train in the USA.

unit trainloads. Lorries complete the job by doing the local delivery and collection of individual containers in the neighbourhood of the inland city depots.

Another form of inter-modal goods transport is possible where the nineteenth-century railway builders left more room under tunnels than they did in Britain. This is the carriage by unit train of complete lorries or lorry trailers between centres in important manufacturing areas and others where the goods are used. Known, not surprisingly, as 'piggyback', it is very popular in North America and growing in Continental Europe.

Piggyback is less economical than the use of containers, because a piggyback train is carrying the dead weight of lorry chassis as well as the goods; but this is becoming less important as the fuel cost of driving a lorry the whole way increases. The convenience of having a lorry or trailer ready to roll straight to its customer when the piggyback train arrives is obvious.

Though every railway tries nowadays to deal with as much of its goods traffic as possible in unit train workings that avoid costly shunting en route, most still handle up to half their freight in individual wagonloads. This is because most still serve small goods depots in every town (British Rail is an exception) and a great many small factories which have their own private sidings.

A way has had to be found to cut the cost of shunting this traffic and to do it more quickly and reliably, both to save manpower and to improve service to the customer. Electronics have provided the answer.

More and more shunting is concentrated in huge yards, the biggest of which can sort over 5,000 wagons a day, where the whole process of shunting is worked out by computers.

Because trains move on fixed tracks and not freely like cars or planes, and because railway working is so strictly timetabled, electronics and automation have done and can still do more to save labour on the railway than in any other form of transport. Far fewer men work on the line nowadays, because machines can do the complete job of removing worn-out track and replacing it with new. They can also keep track in good order; and inspection vehicles equipped with electronic devices can carry out a high-speed but absolutely precise check that the alignment of the rails is correct to a hair's-breadth. Furthermore, the signals and points of as much as 320 km (200 miles) of busy railway, carrying all kinds of different trains, can be comfortably and safely controlled from one push-button signalbox.

The Santa Fe Railway's huge computerized marshalling yard at Barstow, California. Yards like this can sort more than 5,000 wagons a day.

A New Age of the Train?

When fierce air and road competition was forcing US railroads to shut down hundreds of passenger services in the late 1950s and early 1960s, some experts were certain the same thing would happen in the rest of the world, sooner or later. But in 1964 the Japanese made them think again.

As much as 40 per cent of Japan's population and 75 per cent of its industry are packed into only 1 per cent of the country's surface – the coastal area between Tokyo and Osaka, on the biggest of Japan's three main islands, Honshu. The extraordinary post-war industrial development of Japan was naturally concentrated here and, as a result, the existing railway between Tokyo and Osaka was being choked by traffic. But the scope to improve it was limited, partly because it was hemmed in by buildings for much of the way and had many

A Japanese 'Bullet Train' on the new line between Tokyo and Osaka.

In the 1960s, British Rail realized that fast, regular and frequent passenger services were needed to compete with the spreading network of motorways.

curves.

So in 1959 the Japanese took the bold decision to leave the historic Tokyo–Osaka railway to carry only goods and local passenger traffic. For inter-city passenger business they would build a brand-new railway, 515 km (320 miles) long, designed so that its electric trains could run at 210 km/h (130 mph) almost the whole way.

The new Tokyo–Osaka railway, the first of what the Japanese call their *Shinkansen* ('New Fast Railways') started work in October 1964. Within five years it was carrying an average of a quarter of a million passengers a day in trains which were often required to average just over 160 km/h (100 mph) throughout their journeys. This speed and the shape of their streamlined noses quickly earned the *Shinkansen* fliers the nickname of 'Bullet Trains' in the rest of the world.

The first lesson which the Japanese taught the rest of the railway world was that passengers could be won back if the trains were frequent and all of the same standard of comfort and speed. If you decided to make a trip by car, you could choose any hour of the day to start; and if you preferred to fly, there would be little difference in the time it would take to reach your destination, whatever flight you picked. A train service must be just as predictable. The eighty trains which, by 1969, the Japanese were running each way between Tokyo and Osaka

The Japanese 'Bullet Trains' proved that it was safe to run passenger trains at over 160 km/h (100 mph). This British Rail Inter-City 125 can travel at 200 km/h (125 mph) for quite long distances on its way from Newcastle to London.

every day, departed at fixed intervals in every hour, so that you could start your journey with almost as much freedom as in your own car; and the trains were all of the same standard type, running to the same speed.

In Europe British Rail had already realized that services of this kind were needed in the new age of motor transport. In 1966, when they electrified and speeded up the main line from London to Liverpool and Manchester, they re-wrote its timetable to a similar regular-interval pattern and advertised it as a new idea in passenger train service – 'Inter-City'. Though these first Inter-City trains were not as fas as Japan's 'Bullet Trains', by 1970 they were, nonetheless, carrying three out of every four people travelling between London and the two north-western cities.

Since 1966 one European railway after another has followed this model. In several cases they have even given their regular-interval express train services the British 'Inter-City' title. At the same time

European railways have been gradually abandoning the non-standard luxury trains which were put on after the Second World War, like the British Pullmans and the Continental, first-class-only 'Trans-Europ Express'.

In other words, the railways have realized that the urge to travel is now great at all levels of society, and that family car-drivers are a much bigger market than businessmen and others for whom they previously made a special play with extra-fast and comfortable trains.

The other important outcome of the Japanese *Shinkansen* enterprise was proof that trains could be safely operated at over 160 km/h (100 mph) day in and day out. With steam gone and diesel and electric power giving all types of train better acceleration and greater ability to make good speed uphill as well as on the level, there was some room to run Inter-City trains faster. A few European main lines had been built with so few tight curves that railways could afford to rebuild the track to straighten them; that done, the Inter-City trains on these routes could run at an uninterrupted 200 km/h (125 mph) for quite long stretches.

When this BR Advanced Passenger Train enters a curve, its coach bodies tilt to enable the train to take the curve at high speed.

But all too many main lines are either too crowded with traffic or, more often, too frequently curved for trains of the traditional kind to keep up an average of 160 km/h (100 mph). And it is not every government that is willing either to spend huge sums on a new passenger-only, high-speed railway, or to accept the great disturbance of towns and cities involved in finding a path for it. The latter alone would be a great problem in densely-populated countries like Britain, Belgium and Holland, for example.

Some railways, unable to think of building new lines, are trying to get more speed out of the old ones by devising trains that can take curves faster. This is not a question of safety, but of passenger comfort. Railway curves are banked to a degree that suits the average speed of all trains using a line; they cannot be canted just to suit the fastest. So a traditional express train has to take each curve at a speed that does not subject its passengers to unpleasant side-thrust, or too much of what is called centrifugal force. The speed at which there is any risk of derailment is much higher.

To narrow the difference between these two levels of allowable speed, some railways are

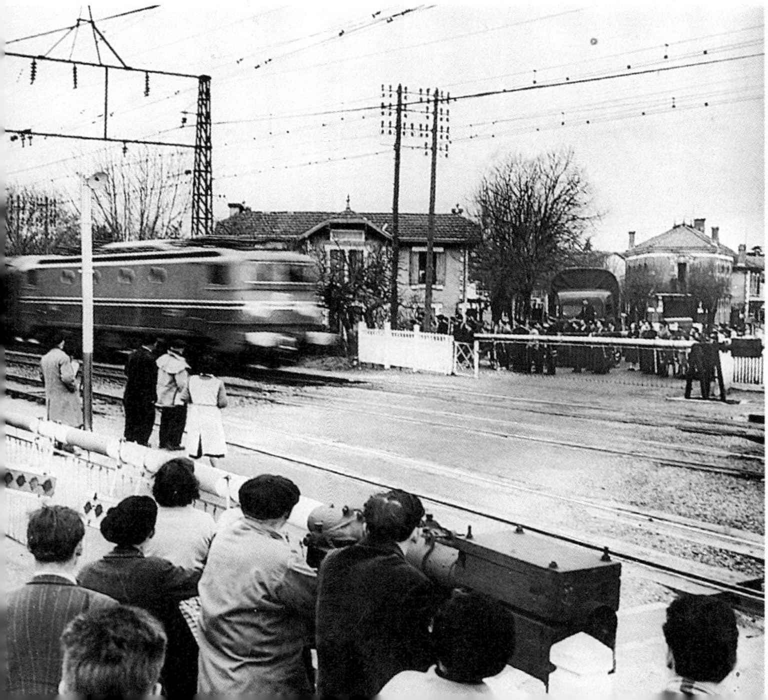

In an experiment in 1955, this French train reached 320km/h (200 mph); but no train has yet been run at this speed on a normal service.

This French TGV train can keep up a steady 260 km/h (160 mph) on the new line from Paris to Lyons.

experimenting with trains which, as soon as they sense they are entering a curve, automatically tilt their coach bodies by a carefully measured degree towards the inside of the bend. In other words, the automatic mechanism adds an extra amount of cant to that which is built into the banking of the track. As a result, such a train can go through a curve as much as 40 per cent faster than an ordinary one and its passengers will feel no difference.

Best-known of these automatic body-tilting designs is British Rail's Advanced Passenger Train, or APT, but others have been developed in Canada, Sweden, Italy and Japan. If they prove reliable, regular 200- and perhaps as much as 240-km/h (125–150-mph) day-to-day Inter-City services will be possible on many more existing railways. But unfortunately none of the complicated tilting mechanisms has yet given foolproof service at high speed.

So, for the present, it is only on brand-new railways that daily rail travel is making solid progress to the 320 km/h (200 mph) which the French achieved in an experiment in 1955. And it is the

French who are nearest to the target.

Because their principal main line from Paris south-eastward to Lyons was getting overcrowded, they, like the Japanese, left it to deal only with slow and local traffic, and built a new and separate express passenger-only railway between the two cities.

This 425-km (264-mile) Paris–Lyons high-speed railway, known as the TGV, was partly opened in 1981 and will come fully into service in 1983. Its trains keep up a steady 260 km/h (160 mph), though they ride so smoothly and quietly that you do not appreciate how fast you are going. Even with a limited service, using only part of their new line, they were soon carrying well over 100,000 passengers a week and had robbed the rival airline of 30 per cent of its passengers.

The French are already planning to build more high-speed TGV railways. One of the important influences on this decision is the fact that the electric TGV train is just as fast for travel between city centres as a plane, yet it uses less fuel per passenger carried. It is more economical still by comparison with road transport.

Worry about future supplies of fuel, and not only its cost, has changed many countries' attitudes to railways since 1973. Everyone agrees that road vehicles are the only practical way of carrying out local transport. But where there is a big flow of passengers or goods between two points, no one seriously disputes that the train, particularly the electric train, can do the job with less use of fuel than any other form of transport, except a slow-moving barge.

An electric express train leaves Rome for Naples, Italy. Where there is a large flow of passengers or goods between two points, a modern electric train is the most efficient means of transporting them, and railway electrification is now a very important industry.

One or two countries, especially Britain, are still worried that the railway costs too much in other ways, and that it must find out how to do its work with fewer staff. But where railways are nationally-owned, most countries are spending more money to improve them than they have since the last war. And one of the world's busier industries in the 1980s is railway electrification.

Glossary

Assembly line A sequence of machines, tools, workers, etc., in a factory, arranged so that at each stage a further process is carried out and the product becomes more complete.

Cant The amount by which one rail on a curve is raised above the other.

Continental Europe The mainland of Europe as distinguished from Britain.

Diesel A type of engine, patented by Dr Rudolf Diesel in 1892, which works by what is known as compression ignition – air is drawn into each of the cylinders and compressed so that its temperature rises high enough for an explosion to occur and power to be created when diesel oil is injected.

Diesel-electric A type of locomotive in which a diesel engine is used to power an electric generator. The electric current produced is then fed to electric motors which move the locomotive.

Electrification The conversion of railway lines for use by electric trains. This involves either laying live rails or installing overhead wires to supply the trains with electric current.

Flange The projecting rim of a wheel which overlaps the rail to prevent the wheel from wandering off the track.

Gauge The distance between the two rails of a railway track. The 'standard' guage – 1.435m (4ft 8½in) – is used by most of the world's railways.

Industrial Revolution The introduction of machinery into manufacturing processes during the eighteenth and nineteenth centuries, first in Britain and then in the rest of Western Europe and the USA.

Loading guage The maximum height and width to which locomotives, coaches and wagons can be built (or loaded) to ensure that they do not hit overbridges, tunnel walls, station platforms, etc.

Marshalling yard An area where goods wagons are collected from their points of origin and formed into trains, where wagons are shunted from one train to another, or where trains are divided up for local delivery of their wagons.

Railroad The American word for railway.

Rolling stock Carriages and wagons.

Trans-Europ Express In 1957 most of the Continental European railways co-operated to run a fleet of international first-class-only trains under this name. To avoid lengthy stops at frontiers, the countries involved agreed that passport and customs examination would be carried out in the trains on the move.

Unit train A complete goods train which travels from its starting point to its destination without being stopped along the route for shunting.

Further reading

Encyclopaedia of Railways edited by O. S. Nock (Octopus, 1977)

The Fastest Trains in the World by G. Freeman Allen (Ian Allan, 1978)

A History of Railways by G. Freeman Allen (Orbis, 1982)

Illustrated History of the Railways of Britain by G. Freeman Allen (Marshall Cavendish, 1979)

Modern Railways by G. Freeman Allen (Hamlyn, 1980)

Railroads of North America by Alan Singer (New English Library, 1977)

Railways Then and Now by O. S. Nock (Paul Elek, 1975)

The Stephensons and Steam Railways by C. C. Dorman (Wayland, 1975)

Index

Picture acknowledgements

The publisher would like to thank all those who supplied pictures on the following pages: British Transport Films 31; British Transport Museum 33; City of Birmingham Museum and Art Gallery 18; Mansell Collection 9, 12; Mary Evans Picture Library 15, 26; Millbrook House Colourviews Picture Library *front cover*, 4 (Science Museum, London), 6, 8 (C. M. Whitehouse), 10 (British Rail), 13, 14 (British Rail), 19 (C. M. Whitehouse), 20, 21, 22 (Cecil J. Allen Collection), 23, 24 (P. B. Whitehouse), 25, 27 (Union Pacific Railroad), 28, 29 (P. J. Howard), 30, 32, 35, 37, 38 (P. J. Howard), 39 (Cecil J. Allen Collection), 40, 41 (P. M. Alexander), 42, 43 (P. B. Whitehouse), 44, 45, 46, 48 (Mrs D. A. Robinson), 49, 51, 52 (G. Freeman Allen), 53 (Santa Fe Railway), 54, 55 (British Rail), 56 (Mrs D. A. Robinson), 57 (Mrs D. A. Robinson), 58 (French Railways), 59 (French Railways), 60; Military Archive & Research Services 17 (Swiss Federal Railways); Peter Newark's Western Americana 11, 16, 34; Science Museum, London 33. The remaining pictures are from the Wayland Picture Library.

To: Daniel Andrews
&
Family

From: Marvin Hall
&
Family

God Bless you Man!!

Back to the Basics

The *Essence* of Communication in Relationships

Dr. Marvin Hall

Order this book online at www.trafford.com
or email orders@trafford.com

Most Trafford titles are also available at major online book retailers.

Printed in the United States of America.

ISBN: 978-1-4269-3843-6 (sc)
ISBN: 978-1-4269-3844-3 (hc)
ISBN: 978-1-4269-3855-9 (e)

Library of Congress Control Number: 2010909980

Trafford rev. 11/04/2010

Trafford PUBLISHING **www.trafford.com**

North America & International
toll-free: 1 888 232 4444 (USA & Canada)
phone: 250 383 6864 • fax: 812 355 4082

Table of Contents

Preface

I've been around leadership development as a practitioner for 43 years. I have had 37 years of experience (in one and only marriage). I still have friends from my grade school days. My college roommate and fraternity brother stay in touch frequently. After reading Marvin's (Dr. Hall) latest book ***Back to the Basics: The Essence of Communication in Relationships,*** it caused me to reflect back on the subject matter in the first four sentences. What I discovered is relationship is the power of being successful in: marriage, raising a family, leadership, and vocational pursuits.

I like the first part of the title ***Back to the Basics,*** because I was reminded that communication makes or breaks relationships. Communication is a lifelong learning opportunity. This book has ten chapters of easy reading, but challenging opportunities to improve your ability in the relationship arena. I could not put it down and read it in one sitting because I was either being reeducated or learning something new. After finishing the book and reading "Some Final Thoughts to Further Understand the Importance of Communication in Relationships," it caused me to start working on my personal development chapter by chapter.

This book is a "keeper." Find out what you are doing that is right for your relationships. Find out about things that you may have been given feedback about but didn't pay attention to. Enjoy the read; you will find that you will be passing on some wisdom nuggets from my friend's book. Last, tell the people in your relationship circle to get their own copy; yours will be marked up.

Ralph Mitchell, Chairman
Nehemiah The Leadership Company

Acknowledgements

I would like to give thanks to all who encouraged and supported my efforts to write this book. First and foremost, a special thanks goes to my wife, Virginia Chris Warren-Hall, for her quiet, but powerful role in encouraging me to complete this book. Thanks also goes to my friends and business partners, Nehemiah, The Leadership Company, Ralph Mitchell and Calvin Riley, for their support and encouragement.

Also, I want to thank Dr. Patricia E. Bonner as contributing editor of this book.

The Purpose of the Book

How we communicate with others directly impacts the relationships we develop in life. The two are inseparable in that they work sequentially to reveal how socialization plays out in life prior to birth while we are still in our mothers' womb and as infants after we are born. Yes, communication and relationship building are garnered and established this early. Foremost, when dealing with the psychology of communication and relationships, it is the intent of this book to simply look at how we as people establish attachments and temperance in relationship building. "Attachment" is defined as having a close emotional bond between individuals. "Temperament" is an individual's behavioral style and how one may emotionally respond by way of action, interaction, and reaction. All of these can influence how we relate to others by way of our relationships which derive from how, what, when, where, why, and to whom we communicate. Now that I am older and have lived through a variety of experiences, I wrote this book with the words serving as my binocular and telescope barometer and thermometer for insight into communication and relationships, because each is within sight and within reach of every individual.

I do believe with all of my being that how each of us communicates directly impacts relationships, given all of the psychological disorders that beset us on a daily basis. I also believe that many disorders can be substantially reduced by understanding how communication and relationships interact. The essence of developing behavior and personality patterns is related to personal experiences, such as attitudes, beliefs, emotions, environment and thoughts, which are all determined by how we communicate in relationships.

Part One:
Communication

Chapter One

The Importance of Active Listening

With the rise of President Barack Obama to presidential power comes a new awareness and excitement about effective communication. From the way people communicate in their families to the difficult communication between the U.S.A. and Iraq – effective communication skills are important and necessary in this 21st century global world.

Many people who experience or have common disorders are affected by communication disorder(s). These disorders may include auditory processing, language barriers, and speech-related problems. The causes of communication disorders may be brain injury, drug abuse, emotional disorders, and neurological disorders, pre or post-natal. According to current research, one in ten Americans of every age, gender, race, and socio-economical status has experienced various types of communication disorders; however, when we look further into the world of relationships and how families utilize communication, there is often a missing component. That component is listening. Listening involves more than one being quiet; it involves "active listening that is so essential to effective communication." Let's look at the following definitions of "active" listening and listening:

The definition of "active" according to Webster's World Thesaurus is busy, lively, energetic, alive, purposeful, and aware.

The definition of "listening," according to Webster's World Thesaurus, is to pay attention, keep one's ears open, be attentive, pick-up on, tune in to, receive, and lend an ear to.

Our ability to understand and communicate effectively is influenced by our internal dialogues. How many times during a conversation have you been so busy talking to yourself about what you are going to say next that you haven't even heard what the other person has been saying for the last five minutes? Some communication experts call this "internal noise." The noise that affects filters can be influenced by emotions, the situation, and your self-concept. Is it any wonder, then, that we all have days when we don't communicate very well? It is extremely important to understand this communication process and learn the skills that help eliminate and increase the effects of your communication skills. The following saying illustrates this: "*I know that you think you understand what I said, but do you also realize that what you heard is not what I meant to say?*" (Loren Ford, 1995).

Common Barriers to Communication

1. **Being overly anxious**: Trying too hard or communicating when upset may cause difficulties.

2. **Being critical or sarcastic**: Seldom does it help a conversation if people feel that they are constantly being judged.

3. **Having a hidden agenda**: It is difficult enough to solve a problem when you have all the information, yet you refuse to work through the problem.

4. **Overreacting and/or Interrupting**: This usually leads to defensiveness and frustration on the part of the speaker.

5. **Stereotyping**: Generalizations are frequently incorrect and only add to other problem-solving situations.

(Some) Methods to Improve Communication

1. **Be more accepting**: We usually want other people to be accepting of our ideas, even when they may not appear to make sense. Try to reciprocate and be accepting of other people's ideas, even when the logic may not be apparent.

2. **Be attentive**: Most of us like to think that what we are talking about is important or meaningful. Paying attention to the person talking says we're listening.

3. **Listen with clarification**: If we pay attention to the non-verbal as well as the words, we may get the real meaning.

4. **Share responsibility for connecting**: To improve communication, both parties need to be actively engaged in making sure that they understand each other.

5. **Wait for the big picture**: When someone is talking and we only notice the particular details, we may miss the main point.

When all of this is done, more times than not, a "promotion of interaction" is achieved. Promoting interaction can lead to establishing clear channels of communication in relationships. When people are linked to one another, they begin to work together and relate personally to one another. Thus, they learn how to listen "actively" and become effective in the communication process by using insightfulness and sensitivity.

Chapter Two

Conceptual Model for "Active" Listening

Conceptual Model for Listening

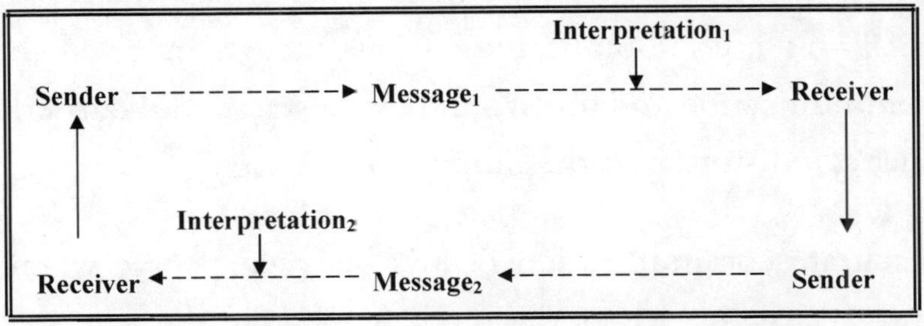

The Conceptual Model for Listening helps you to be sensitive to perceiving messages that are consistent with your own value system. You may misperceive or even fail to understand messages that are different from your own attitudes, beliefs, cognitive style, and opinions. Thus, the way you send and/or receive a message can very well be distorted. An understanding of the conceptual model allows you to listen "actively" for the full message.

You can also easily understand the complexity of communication by considering the example of the game of passing a single message through a series of individuals. In this game, one person thinks of a message and in turn whispers it to another. The next person attempts to whisper the same message to another person, who does the same, passing it to as many people as possible. When the last person tells the entire group what his or her version of the message is, it is usually very different from the original message. How does a relatively simple message become distorted when conveyed to another person? To understand this, you must look at the various factors involved in communication and understand the obstacles and barriers that can distort even the simplest of messages.

Accurate communication occurs between people when the receiver interprets the sender's message the way the sender intended it. Difficulties in communication arise when the receiver imparts to the message a meaning that is not intended. When the sender attempts to convey a message, the receiver interprets the message before he or she can respond to it. All forms of communication require some degree of interpretation; an individual must construe, understand, and attach individual meaning to a message. It is through this act of interpretation that communication can become distorted. The process of interpretation is always filtered through our individual biases, expectations, and prejudices. When information is transmitted, the listener tends to accept what seems to fit into his or her belief system and sometimes rejects or distorts information that is inconsistent with these beliefs. Also, people are sometimes so sure they know what the other person is going to say that they distort the incoming message to match their expectations. For example, if a man who has very low self-esteem asks his boss for a raise, he may take the boss's statement, "I'll have to give it some thought" as a sign of refusal when the boss has said that he wants to think about it. "A common problem in communication occurs when the receiver understands the words of the message but fails to recognize the sender's underlying meaning." (Schmolling, Paul Jr., Youkeles, Merrill, & Burger, William R., *Human Services in Contemporary America* 3rd Edition (1993).

This is extremely important because it is imperative to find ways of relating the concerns of one individual to the concerns and struggles of another. This also provides further opportunities for mutual support and helps to develop a feeling of advocacy, which is the highest form of supporting another person and learning how to communicate by listening "actively." When people go through struggles, disappointments, and unexpected tragedies, they hope that their mates will be supportive by listening, consoling, and helping them craft a strategy for survival.

> *"The deepest hunger of the human soul is to be understood. The deepest hunger of the human body is for air. If you can listen to another person, in depth, until they feel understood, it's the equivalent of giving them air."*
>
> *---Author unknown*

Chapter Three

The Way Dominant Senses Can Influence "Effective" Communication

How Our Dominant Sense(s) Influence Our Perceptions and Sensations

It is very important for you to find out your dominant sense because usually the manner in which we communicate may depend on which sense(s) you utilize the most. We learn and depend on our senses to process information; thus, this may be the difference in just communicating with someone and *effectively* communicating with him or her.

Many problems in communication stem from a lack of your understanding of your dominant sense; this is shown many times by your choice of words and interpretations.

Types of Dominant Senses

Visually Oriented Person: I see what you mean, but I think your attitude is crystal clear.

Touch Oriented Person: I feel good about what you are saying, but your words seem out of touch with your real attitude.

Hearing Oriented Person: I hear what you're saying, but I don't like the sound of your voice.

Quarrels and differences of opinion are inevitable when people communicate in relationships. In fact, problem-solving situations will arise and when they do, the answer to a problem or problems may be a positive interaction because more times than not, it's the differences that can lead to an understanding more than the correct answer to a problem. This can be very important to understand in relationships because the problem that causes the conflict may evolve and transfer into a beneficial experience rather than a conflict that may exacerbate things. It is so important to utilize conflicts to understand people in a relationship.

Sometimes, addressing a problem comes in the form of talking to a person's feelings rather than the problem and/or the source of the problems. When you get a bad "vibe" from someone, that feeling from the other person may be legitimate; thus, the problem can become worse because the feelings are inappropriately addressed. This is done by telling the other person not to feel the way he or she feels. Now the original problem may be the source of the problem because now the person feels that he or she is being told how to feel.

A common scenario is when there is a crisis of grief and/or bereavement. Family and friends may say, "Get over it and get on with your life," when your feelings are not being taken into consideration. They may be only looking at the behavior rather than the cause of the behavior.

Chapter Four

Using "I" Messages Rather Than "You" Messages

Reflective listening occurs when you can force yourself to listen before you speak. This can be very hard to do in the heat of an argument or disagreement because it has to be done to help obtain and maintain constructive and productive conflict resolution techniques.

In the heat of an argument, people have a tendency to defend their positions. Reflective listening again forces us to control how we respond to others. So, instead of being defensive when a partner accuses you of making decisions, you can say the following: "It sounds like you feel angry and hurt when I make major decisions without speaking to you." If the accusation or disagreement is handled in the above manner, first it lets the person understand that you have listened to what he or she has said and that no matter "how and what" the person has said, your thoughts and feelings are important to you. Second, it allows you to clarify until you have truly understood why the person thinks and feels the way he or she does. This form of "reflective listening" can help solve problems that can continue to cause a continuum of problem-solving. So give credence to someone's feelings without addressing the problem directly. If this is done properly, rapport and understanding of feelings become primary, and everything else becomes secondary because many times feelings serve as a precursor to understanding and problem-solving. Lastly, feelings are temporary and contribute to your happiness intermittently, but emotions are permanent and contribute to your joy everyday and throughout life.

Rule #1: "I" Messages Should Be Used Rather Than "You" Messages

"I" messages focus on the husband rather than the wife because if the husband speaks to his wife, he represents the "I" messages, and the wife represents the "You" messages.

For example, if your husband says something that angers you, you may say, "*You (wife) make me angry when you say that to me.*" This may be the wrong way to "fight fair." Instead you should say, *"I feel angry when you say that.*" This is an "I" message. The "I" message here focuses on the "you" and allows the other person a chance to evaluate, identify, and recognize what he is saying without feeling the need to defend him or herself. One way this can be accomplished is by people developing their versatility in listening "actively" more to others so that they really feel that others truly understand their point of view.

Notes

Notes

Part Two

Companionship

Chapter Five

Unhealthy Relationships vs. Healthy Relationships

Every relationship is unique, and you may have your own way of knowing when a relationship is right for you. Even when a relationship is going well, it is important that you continue to put effort into keeping it healthy, and don't take the relationship for granted. You should also be aware of what you need in a relationship, as well as what the other person needs. This way, relationships that you are involved in have the best chance of growing and continuing to be strong and healthy.

Some analysts suggest that relationships fall into one of two major categories: "person-oriented" relationships and "need-oriented" relationships. The distinction lies, primarily, on the focus both parties place on the relationship (Chambers, 2005).

In a "person-oriented" relationship, the focus is on the people involved. There, it appears that people are bonded more from a mutual like and enjoyment of each other than anything else. In a "need oriented" relationship, the focus is on meeting one another's needs and expectations. There, the bonding appears to be based more on an "I'll do for you, and you do for me" philosophy.

Healthy people tend to gravitate to "person-oriented" relationships (Chambers, 2005). Because healthier individuals are so self-sufficient and self-contained to begin with, they seem to be more attracted to relationships wherein factors of compatibility and likeability are paramount (Chambers, 2005). Healthy people are not looking for a relationship where they need to be taken care of; instead, they look for a relationship where they can find sharing and the full enjoyment of another person. Unhealthier individuals, because they lack emotional self-sufficiency, gravitate more to "need-oriented" relationships. Here, the goal is to find a partner who can take care of their lack of emotional self-sufficiency.

In some cases, the "need-orientation" of a relationship appears quite conscious and patently obvious, for example, the divorcee with three children looking for someone to support her or the rich executive who simply seeks a younger attractive, social friend. But in most cases, the needs involved run a bit deeper, psychologically speaking, and are unrecognized, even by the parties involved (Chambers, 2005). Here, there is the whole gamut of needs most people bring into a relationship. Some are the need to reduce our insecurity and loneliness; the need to live up to social familial expectations; the need to relieve some of our daily burdens; and so many more. However, mainly the "need-oriented" relationship is seen as a place where a person expects to, and on some level, needs to be taken care of by his or her partner. The problem is, in most cases of a need-oriented relationship, our partner is expecting the same thing that he or she has given in the relationship to be returned. On the surface, the differences between these two categories of relationships are subtle. In the "need-oriented" relationship your spouse or lover might say to you, "I love you because of what you do for me," whereas in the "person-oriented" relationship your spouse or lover might say, "I love you just for you."

Below the surface, however, the differences become more pronounced, particularly when one examines the kinds of feelings each tends to produce. "Need-oriented" relationships tend to produce a host of uncomfortable feelings. They are usually characterized as having a high degree of expectations, obligations, duties, "guilt-trips," pressures, and demands. Such stresses are based on the fact that "needs" have become a critical issue in the relationship. One of the partners or both have come to expect that the other partner should meet their expectations. With these needs come a lot of pressuring, demands, and expectations. When these needs are not met, resentment, hurt feelings and distancing are sure to follow.

An unhealthy relationship occurs when there is an imbalance of intimacy. There are several signs that signal to people that they are in an unhealthy relationship. An example of an unhealthy relationship is when a person focuses more on the other partner and neglects totally his or her own feelings to the detriment of the relationship. One may also feel pressure to change to meet the other person's standards, one may be afraid to disagree, and one's ideas may be criticized. Or, he may also pressure the other person to meet his standards and criticize his ideas. He may also focus on another person only and neglect himself, or he may focus only on himself and neglect the other person. One of the individuals has to justify what he does, where he goes, and whom he sees. In this type of imbalanced relationship one of the individuals makes all of the decisions and controls everything without listening to the other's input. The other person feels unheard and is unable to control anything without listening to the other's input and is unable to communicate what he desires; thus one individual has less of a voice and power in the relationship.

Two Basic Areas That Can Determine the Outcome of a Relationship

Two basic areas can determine the outcome of a relationship, "private" and "public responses." When you are in an intimate relationship, you must be cautious of "put downs" or saying things that are condescending to your friend or mate when the environment you just left was full of romanticism and praises for the other person or persons. Another scenario is when you are in a public setting and your friend or mate diminishes you in some way. This is certainly one of the easiest ways to obtain, maintain, and sustain an unhealthy relationship, regardless of the type of relationship.

The second area is the voices from behind. Our families of origin also play a large part in how we communicate. Every family has its own style of communicating, for example, how they argue, show anger or affection, and how they determine which feelings are "allowable" to express. This style will vary from family to family. We take these dynamics with us into our relationships, and they will likely differ from the communication styles that our partner learned in his or her family. The task for your relationship is to negotiate your own communication style within your partnership. These styles and differences will lead to a deeper understanding of communication and can indicate where your partner is coming from. They are not intended to be used as excuses for avoiding change. In a relationship, each partner has the right to ask for what he or she wants or needs, and each partner has the right to decide how willing or able he or she is to make changes. In order to explore these issues, you must be assertive in expressing your needs. A willingness to explore these issues is a sign of a healthy relationship, or an inability to do so may be a signal that a bigger change is in order.

"Words of Wisdom"

The paradox of our time is that we have taller buildings, but shorter tempers; wider freeways, but narrower viewpoints. We buy more, but enjoy less. We have bigger houses and smaller families; more convenience, but less time. We have more advanced degrees, but less good judgment; more medicine, but less wellness.

We have multiplied our possessions, but reduced our values. We have higher incomes, but lower morals.

We have been all the way to the moon and back, but have trouble crossing the street to meet a new neighbor. We've conquered outer space, but inner space is still a mystery to too many of us.

We have cleaned up the air, but polluted the soul; split the atom, but not our prejudices.

We talk too much, love too seldom, and hate too often.

These are times of steep profits and shallow relationships; world peace, but domestic warfare; more leisure, but less fun; two incomes and more divorce.

It is a time when there is much in the show window and nothing in the stockroom; a time when technology can bring a letter to you in seconds, and you can choose either to make a difference or just hit delete.

--Author unknown

Gender-Based Communication: Talking across Two Different Cultures

Deborah Tannen, a professor of linguistics at Georgetown University, wrote a fascinating and widely acclaimed book entitled, You Just Don't Understand: Women and Men in Conversation (1990), which deals with the complexities of communication between the sexes. Drawing upon a distinguished research career, Tannen presents vivid examples of how women and men are socialized to relate and dialogue with others in such pronouncedly different ways that the two sexes often stumble in their efforts to connect. In various public lectures as well as in her book, which was a national best-seller, Tannen maintains that the sexes are, in a very real sense, communicating from the perspective of two different cultures.

Tannen further contends that men use language to convey information, achieve status in a group, challenge others, and keep from getting pushed around. Women, on the other hand, use language to achieve and share intimacy with others, promote closeness and equality in a group, and prevent others from pushing them away. Stated another way, men often grow up thinking that people will try to push them around, if given a chance, and often enter into conversations about who is one-up and who is one-down. From this perspective, communication becomes something of a contest in which a man endeavors to avoid being put in a one-down position. A man operating within this framework might be expected to be overly sensitive about asking advice or directions, being told to do something, or engaging in any other behavior or dialogue that even remotely resembles being in a one-down or pushed-around position. Tannen illustrates this point with the example of a man whose wife has requested that he do a specific task around the house. Rather than complying with her request immediately, he might wait and let some time pass before responding, so it will not appear as if he is being told what to do. In contrast, women are not typically socialized to use language as a defensive weapon to avoid being dominated or controlled. Rather, their concern is often to use dialogue as a way to get close to another person – and as a way to judge how close to or distant they are from a valued partner. Tannen has some particularly enlightening things to say about women and men engaging in what she calls "troubles talk."

She says, "Women and men are both frustrated by the other's way of responding to their expression of troubles. And they are further hurt by the other's frustration. If women resent men's tendency to offer solutions to problems, men complain about women's refusal to take action to solve the problems they complain about. Since many men see themselves as problem solvers, a complaint or a problem is a challenge in their ability to think of a solution, just as a woman being presented with a broken bicycle or stalling car poses a challenge to her ingenuity in fixing it. But whereas many women appreciate help in fixing mechanical equipment, few are inclined to appreciate help in "fixing" emotional troubles," (Tannen, 1996).

A woman may talk about her problems to foster a sense of rapport and to achieve a feeling of "I am not alone." What she wants is a response that says, "I understand; I have been there, too." For a woman, "troubles talk is intended to reinforce a rapport by sending the message, "We're the same; you're not alone" (p. 53). Such a response would put both communicators on an equal footing, thus allowing intimacy to be built around equality. However, when a man responds with advice when his partner is only looking for understanding, his response frames him "as more knowledgeable, more reasonable, more in control – in a word, one-up." (Tannen, 1996). And this contributes to the distancing effect. Tannen tells women to minimize this relationship-eroding influence by telling their partners that when dealing with emotional troubles, they do not want solutions, just someone to listen.

Chapter Six

Male vs. Female Perspectives on Intimacy

Intimate relationships usually involve three basic components: emotional attachment, feelings of affection, and love. Intimacy occurs when you communicate important feelings and information to your significant other (many times self-disclosure). Intimacy, more times than not, may be sharing deep concern in an emotional manner rather than in a physical way. This is very important because men usually think of intimacy in a physical sense, whereas many women think of it in a romantic sense. Therefore, there is a chance for conflicts and/or misinterpretations to arise in relationships between men and women. One gender can and will communicate opposing messages and not realize that intimacy for men can be expressed differently than for women.

Intimacy has been researched over the years. One would assume that this simple concept is understood by the vast majority who are involved in relationships. However, in these times there seems to be widespread misconception of intimacy in relationships. Also, this may contribute heavily to failed relationships and unhappy people over time.

The fulfillment of psychological needs, such as sharing feelings and gaining reassurance in the relationship, may create intimacy. Interdependence between individuals, each of whom has a meaningful and enduring influence on the other, can also be considered.

Note:

Emotional closeness is very important to a woman. It makes her feel loved, understood, and secure. To facilitate this kind of closeness a man will need to practice reflective listening. He must learn to be non-judgmental through reflecting her feelings back to her. Although he may want to fix her feelings, he must resist that temptation. She doesn't want him to fix anything; she just wants him to be understanding.

You should make a special effort to get in touch with your own feelings, then share them with your significant other. You may be surprised at how *intimate* that feels.

Thought for the Day:

> **Sex is used differently by men and women in a love relationship. Many women view sharing as being close and men view being close as something sexual. Women view sex as one way of being close and too many men view it as the only way to be close. For women, tenderness, touching, talking, and sex go together. For some men, sex is sufficient, especially if they do not know how to relate in other forms of intimacy.**
>
> *--H. Norman Wright*

One would assume that this simple concept of intimacy is understood by the vast majority of those who have ever experienced a truly loving relationship. However, it would seem that there are just as many, if not more, who remain totally oblivious to intimacy being anything other than satisfying their own sexual needs. Perhaps this seemingly widespread misconception provides a partial answer as to why there are many failed relationships, unhappy couples, and divorces in our generation today.

Chapter Seven

Say "No" to Happiness-Busters

We make our own happiness, but we can unmake it as well or allow others to do the job for us. Be prepared to ward off the following:

- **Esteem-Snatchers**. They are people who are critical of you and your goals. People who do nothing but complain are guaranteed to drain the happiness right out of you. If they're relatives, curtail the time you spend together. If it's a spouse or significant other, try counseling.
- **Unfavorable Comparisons**. Another person's happiness is impossible to quantify. Why bother?

All comparisons do are divert time and energy from your own pursuits.

- **Unrealistic Expectations**. If you expect a steady diet of happiness, you're sure to be disappointed because there are plenty of times when life hurts. The best thing you can do to invite happiness is to respect its ebbs and flows. Accept the pain; experience it fully with the knowledge that, in time, happiness will return to you.

--Dr. Joyce Brothers, 2000

Application

Aim to Be Happy

Write the words "I intend to be happy" on a piece of paper and stick it on the bathroom mirror so that you see it every morning. It will remind you to cherish everything in your day that contributes to happiness: spending a special moment with a child, drinking a cup of your favorite coffee, joking with a co-worker, or saving a rosebush from destruction. Happiness hides in life's small details. If you're not looking, it becomes invisible. Remember, you have a duty to notice.

Explore Your Spirituality

Studies show that people with strong religious faith and affiliations are happier than those without such faith, and they also regain happiness more quickly after experiencing a crisis. You don't need to wait for a strong sense of commitment to become involved. Most churches, synagogues and mosques have membership committees that will make you feel at home. Behavior follows belief.

If you're not interested in organized religion, you can still become conscious of the spirit. You should tune into the feeling that you are part of something greater. Slow down and look within. Set aside 15 minutes a day to simply sit and listen to the silence, perhaps in a retreat in your own back yard.

Keep Fit

Eating right and exercising add to our joy in life. Exercise releases endorphins, the pleasure chemicals of the body. But there are also great health and happiness benefits in simple activity – like walking half an hour a day. Walking gives you time to observe the world, think about the pleasures of the day, and work on building your gratitude quotient. It's where the mind and body come together.

Know What to Change

Happiness is a balance between making life go your way and accepting what comes your way. How does one distinguish between the two? Give serious thought to your job, relationships, and other important issues. Objectively, consider what *can* be fixed, what's best to accept, and what *must* be changed.

Like Yourself

Naturally, happy people think well of themselves, no matter what their level of success, because they don't depend on others for approval. Honestly, evaluate your strengths and weaknesses. Realize that your weaknesses are part of being human. Forgive yourself for mistakes; everyone makes them. Set realistic goals. Applaud each positive achievement, no matter how small. Ask close friends and loved ones to give you support or be your own cheering section. Most importantly, accept your feelings. When you stop berating yourself, you're free to experience other emotions – like happiness.

Pursue Your Interests

When you're intensely involved in an activity you enjoy, such as drawing, knitting, woodworking, programming a computer, or playing a sport – you experience a state of absorption called "flow." Psychologist Mihaly Csikszentmihalyi, an expert on flow, calls it a "state of effortless action" in which you and the task at hand become one. Total engagement occurs when something you are genuinely interested in produces a sense of contentment and accomplishment.

Reach Out to Others

People involved in close social relationships are often happier than those who are isolated. But it's possible to be isolated even when you're surrounded by people – if you aren't communicating. Tell the people you love how much you love them every single day. Initiate new friendships and nurture old ones. Build good relationships and rapports in the workplace. People are happiest on the job when they get along, so get to know your co-workers. Finally, get involved in at least one volunteer activity. When you help others, you feel good.

Seize the Sunny Side

Optimism is the belief that things are likely to go well. It encourages resiliency, enthusiasm and perseverance – the very skills we need to be happy from day to day. Studies have found that optimists actually are more realistic than others and more willing to accept bad news, probably because they believe they can make things better.

If you're the kind of person who notices mainly the negatives, alter your focus. You can do this by keeping a diary of each day's positive experiences. Be wary of helpless feelings, the underpinnings of pessimism.

Start Today

It's common to think, for example, that "I'll be happy when I meet the right person," or "I'll be happy when I get a raise." But to be happy, it's necessary to "seize the day" because the only guaranteed time we've got to change our lives is now.

Take a Gratitude Inventory

Sages have noted that happiness comes from being content with what you've got. But in today's world, we're not encouraged to value what we have. There are plenty of courses on how to achieve success, but few on how to be grateful. So we have to teach ourselves how to be grateful.

--Dr. Joyce Brothers, 2000

Along with saying "no" to happiness-busters, one has to look at interaction as a socialization process which involves person-oriented skills along with support systems. However, another salient tool that is more people-oriented is optimism. Optimism can serve as the bridge for happiness. It helps you to obtain joy, which is a permanent fixture, whereas happiness can be temporary. Optimism enhances the feeling that you have personal control over the circumstances in your life and relationships. This is when a person develops a "hardy personality and/or hardiness." Hardiness is characterized by a high level of commitment and a view that change can be an opportunity for growth and control.

Notes

Notes

Notes

Part Three
Character

Chapter Eight

Birth Order and Personality or What Makes You the Way You Are

Birth order can influence many aspects in our lives, mainly relationships. The innate qualities we learn and possess because of the order in which we are born are shocking. Without knowledge of these behaviors, many relationships are doomed from the beginning. Even though all cases do not follow the birth order system, most do. Our personalities are strongly influenced by the order of our birth, which in turn affects the types of jobs we get to the kind of relationships we hold on to. Most people are not aware of the impact it has on their lives until it is too late and they are headed for divorce or separation.

Characteristics of First-borns:

To begin with, first-born children are natural leaders. They do not take criticism well and are perfectionists. First-born daughters seem to have strong maternal instincts. They take charge of situations and sometimes can be intimidating to others. Usually, they are very responsible and follow rules to a fault. They have very strong opinions and do not like to hear the word "no." They like to finish all tasks at hand, and they usually do them well. On the other hand, this personality also shows moodiness and the inability to take orders from others.

- First-born children begin life with no competition for parental attention. They also have the most inexperienced parents. The first-born is a "guinea pig" for the siblings who follow.
- First-born children are often "placed on a throne."
- When another sibling enters the family, the first-born is suddenly dethroned.
- After dethronement, a first-born may attempt to once again become the center of attention by displaying positive or negative behavior.

- First-borns tend to be steady, responsible, dependable, and conformists. They get along well with authority figures.
- Another key fact regarding first-borns is that they are not allowed to be children for very long. They soon assume the responsibility of helping with the second-born. This is the opposite of last-borns who are most often encouraged to be children for too long.
- First-borns find younger siblings looking up to them, depending on them. They learn responsibility early.

Characteristics of Only Children:

Onlies have inexperienced parents. Parental anxiety may contribute to feelings of insecurity for a child who is the only child. Onlies may feel lonely and resent not having brothers or sisters. Other characteristics follow:

- Surrounded by experienced adults, onlies feel incompetent.
- The lack of siblings also encourages responsibility because there are no older siblings to lean on. They often quickly become self-reliant.

- Onlies may feel lonely and resent not having siblings.
- The lack of siblings means less opportunities to learn sharing and self-assertiveness.
- Onlies have more experience relating to those much older or younger than to their peers.

Characteristics of Second Children

- The second-born asks, "Do I want to be like him or her?" to which the reply is almost always, "No, I want to do my own thing." The second-born's personality is often formed in relationship to the first-born. A second-born "bounces off" the first-born, sometimes as an opposite.
- If the first-born is a "pleaser" who does what mom and dad want, the second may be a rebel. The second often finds identity by bouncing off the first.
- The second child is born behind and runs hard to catch up. If a second-born senses the older is stronger or smarter, he or she will typically develop to show mom and dad what D's and F's are all about. If the older is neat and clean, the latter may be messy and careless.

Characteristics of Middle Children

The middle child is described as a "people pleaser." Usually, as a child he or she is the peacekeeper. The middle children have a tendency to change their ideas based on what they think people think about them. If they are with a firstborn, they can sometimes pick up his or her characteristics, which causes a power struggle. Sometimes, however, they may be dominated and give in. A middle child, paired with another middle child, quite often is not a good pair. They both want to please the other until no one is happy. A middle child is indentified as the following:

- The third of four children is a middle child, but so is the third of five or six.
- In many families the second is a middle.
- Middles as a group are the most diverse and hardest to predict.
- A middle child is denied both the privileges of the oldest or the special treatment afforded the youngest.
- A middle may be uncertain of his or her place and feel neglected and unloved.
- Middles sometimes feel parents pay them less attention than the older and younger siblings. Less

fuss is made of them, and it's harder for them to define a unique place within the family.

- Middles that grow up with bothers, younger and older siblings are often more sociable. They are also often peacemakers and good at compromise.
- Middles quickly learn how to handle rivalry and competition. These are coping skills an only child or last child will find more difficult to learn.

Characteristics of Youngest Children (The Last-Borns)

The last-born, which is the baby of the family, tends to be fun-loving. Last-borns find fun in everything they do. They tend to want a lot of attention and find many ways of getting it. But with some of their relationships, when the fun is gone, they are gone. In my research, I found that a last-born with a first-born is a good match because the last-born puts excitement into the first-born's life. On the other hand, the first-born can teach the last-born financial responsibility and let him or her know when to be serious. Characteristics of last-borns are listed below:

- The youngest is in many ways similar to an only child, but has siblings to observe and learn from.

- The youngest is often "spoiled" by parents and other siblings.
- The youngest may lack self-reliance, act the "baby," and succeed in having things done for him.
- The youngest may typically receive inconsistent treatment. Cuddled and spoiled one minute, they're often put down and made fun of the next.
- The youngest are often pre-judged. Teachers compare them to older siblings.
- The youngest are less self-reliant than other birth order groups. But they often learn to manipulate others into doing what they can do for themselves.

Exceptions to the Rules:

- If you are five or more years older or younger than your nearest sibling, you very likely have many of the psychological experiences of the first-born. Those who are ten or more years older or younger share much in common with only children.
- A first-born boy or girl in a family, even though not the first child, may receive treatment much like a first-born.

- Blended families caused by second or third marriages are more complex to understand. Each set of firsts, middles, and lasts pairs off in natural competition. Once everyone is again assured of their place, they feel more secure.
- If children are very young when the family blends, the odds are better that they will build solid relationships as brothers and sisters.

Summation

There are so many different combinations that it is hard to predict the behavior of someone "only" according to his or her birth order. We may factor in the effects of birth order personalities in order to better understand people's behavior in a relationship. It is not "set in stone" that everyone follows the same path, but for the most part we tend to show some signs of our birth order. Understanding this can help avoid problems when in the corporate world, church, home, school or any place and any type of interaction.

Chapter Nine

Intra-personal Perspectives about Effective Communication and Relationships

Relationships are very tricky. People are often indecisive and don't like telling others exactly what they want or like. We are all individuals, and we have different ways of responding to our environment. That's why relationships are difficult to maintain in a healthy manner.

Psychologists or counselors who deal with divorce situations often talk about the fact that what originally attracts people to each other is the same thing that eventually causes the break-up. It is often said that "opposites attract," and this is quite true. Our opposite often represents our shadow or hidden personality, and we instinctively know that if we could get in touch with this part of our personality, we would be more whole.

For example, people who are quiet are often attracted to people who are more vocal or "loud." This is due to the recognition of something they lack in their own personality. It could be that they think the person will bring them out a bit, or they will help them relax more, but they often long for that which they do not have. When these factors of attraction turn to antagonism in a break-up, what becomes apparent is nothing else is holding the relationship together. If this is the case, then very soon the loudness or quietness of the other will begin to irritate the other until there will be nothing else to sustain this relationship. What happens is that the relationship degenerates into criticism, usually of the things that first attracted them to each other; then arguments, regret, panic, and blame become the norm. This is due to frustration that the relationship they sought is not working out the way they had envisioned. The tragedy is that this is so common. The reality is that attractions, passion and sex usually get in the way of rational decisions, and all too many of us end up with relationships that are not satisfying or long-lasting.

The truth is that opposites do attract, but relationships only work out well if our goals and values are synchronized with those of our partners'. The major challenge in this is that most people do not have goals and may even have difficulty verbalizing their values. Opposites attract, but only in temperament. Psychologists use a system of 'preferences' that explain how we each react to our external environment and the behavior we exhibit. These preferences are based on the following factors: extraversion, introversion, thinking, feeling, intuition, and sensing. We all use a combination of these but have built-in inclinations for those that we prefer to use most often. Each one has a preferred attitude, such as extraversion or introversion, which we use to relate to the outside world.

Researchers have discovered that people in the world can be divided into two different behavioral attitudes, which are extraversion and introversion. There are people whose behavioral preference is for extraversion, which means that they take their energy from people and things externally; other people with a behavioral preference for introversion take their energy from inside themselves. They have no great need of externalizing their thoughts or feelings. Both types have very different ways of relating to people. The extraverts are quite happy thinking out loud and meeting lots of people. The introverts keep their own counsel and rarely care to impact others' opinions.

This combination can work very well provided neither is extreme. If one or both are an extreme of either type, they will probably drive each other mad. We can all display both introversion and extraversion when required in given situations, but each one of us has a preference for using one more than the other, most of the time. In addition to introversion and extraversion, people use "thinking" or "feeling" processes in how they prefer to deal with situations. It is easy to see how these two styles complement each other; however, again, it is also easy to see that if either is at the extreme end of the scale, the relationship will not work at all.

If each recognizes the other's needs, then the relationship will be successful. Once they have learned to compromise and deal with each other's tolerance levels, they can make plans to accommodate them.

There are three critical areas to foster good communication and relationship. The following ACT Model helps with obtaining and maintaining good solid relationships:

Three Critical Areas for Any Relationship

A. **AWARENESS:** Maintaining an awareness of the problem and pressures that involve communication with others can help you insure that situations do not worsen to the point that you feel helpless, hopeless, and desperate. Others should realize that problems often seem bigger than they really are; therefore, they should be careful not to dismiss problems as trivial.

C. **COMMUNICATION:** This is one of the most important principles. Clear, effective communication between partners and others is the key to maintaining awareness and providing the guidance and support they require. Without good communication, others can only guess what is happening within the relationship, and usually such guesses are wrong.

T. **TRUST:** An atmosphere of mutual trust facilitates communication and decreases the likelihood that you will feel alienated and helpless. You must perceive family and friends as reliable, stable, and trustworthy if you need to turn to them for help in times of trouble. Others also must be willing to trust because trust allows them to develop the healthy independence necessary to cope with life's trials and tribulations.

"You simply can't think efficiency with people. You think effectiveness with people and efficiency with things. I've tried to be "efficient" with a disagreeing or disagreeable person and it simply doesn't work. I've tried to give ten minutes of "quality time" to a child or an employee to solve a problem, only to discover *efficiency* creates new problems and seldom resolves the deepest concern."

--Author Unknown

Chapter Ten

Interpersonal Perspectives about Effective Communication and Relationships (Haptonomy)

There are many reasons that human development has been studied throughout the years. As humans we undergo processes of development that affect us throughout life. Over time, researchers have unlocked information we deal with from conception to death. Some of those areas of development are assessed by researching three domains. Domains are areas that primarily make up human development and growth. Cognitive development involves our thinking and problem solving, which includes alteration in our creativity, language, memory, perceptions and reasoning. Physical development primarily involves height, weight, brain structure, muscles, glands, health, motor skills, and other sense organs. Psychosocial development involves the development of personality and social skills. This includes a person's style of how he or she handles emotional responses and interpersonal skills as he or she relates to self-concept and reacts to social circumstances and situations in life. These three domains extend throughout one's life in stages that develop over time in the individual's behavior, body structure and thought processes. These stages are as follows:

1. Prenatal Development - Conception to Birth
2. Infancy and Toddlerhood Development - Birth to 3 years old
3. Early Childhood Development - 3 to 6 years old
4. Middle Childhood Development - 6 to 11 years old
5. Adolescence Development - 11 to about 20 years old
6. Young Adulthood Development - 20 to 40 years old
7. Middle Adulthood Development - 40 to 65 years old
8. Late Adulthood Development - 65 years old and beyond

Also, looking at the context of the three primary domains of human development, it is critical to examine how humans evolve and how behavior and attitudes are transferred. Much of this is directly related to the socialization of intrapersonal, interpersonal, and group dynamics.

Another salient aspect of human development is the heredity vs. environmental experiences in life. Many say that the two are intertwined or interrelated. With the aforementioned research and scientific study, there is another area that is really fascinating. It is call haptonomy. This is the study of the womb of the mother as the environment. This is fascinating because the infant develops a relationship with the mother and father while inside the womb. It becomes obvious that from the time we are born to the time we die, people observe how we act. But it is also important to understand that prior to birth, during the prenatal period, the baby is also developing relationships to the outside world.

Can We Talk to the Unborn?

Research has now established that we begin to communicate with other humans before we are born. This is call haptonomy. It is the scientific study of our ability to communicate at a deep level. But unlike talking, haptonomic communication combines words, thoughts, and feelings. It has been described as a "combination of listening and feeling," "spontaneous empathy," "psychoactivity contact," or "the science of affectivity." But whatever the name, it is a special sort of relating, one human being to another.

Dr. Ludvig Janus is a well-known clinical developmental psychologist from Heidelberg, Germany. In his book, The Enduring Effects of the Prenatal Experience (Northvale, New Jersey: Jason Aronson 1997), Dr. Janus cites research demonstrating that a communications link between the unborn child and other humans is very real indeed. He shows how it is possible for parents to establish such a relationship.

He also describes the results of establishing this link for both child and mother. Another major figure in this new field of research is Dr. Frans Veldman, who is head of the International Centre for Research and Development of Haptonomy in Oms, Ceret, France and chief organizer of the first UNESCO conference on haptonomy in 1990. In experiments conducted by Dr. Veldman, it was discovered that during the final trimester of pregnancy, if a father places his hand upon the abdomen of his pregnant wife, an extraordinary thing happens. Watching under ultrasound imaging, the unborn child responds to the invitation to relate, moves itself toward his hand resting on the mother's belly and snuggles into it. When the father's hand is taken away, the baby moves. There is a distinct desire for the unborn baby to establish communication or contact in the womb.

This phenomenon was also discovered in the 1980's by Dr. Eric Reinhold of Stuttgart, Germany. Dr. Reinhold humorously observed, "Without saying a word, mother wakes you up, the first time now, but it won't be the last." (Veldman, F. 1994) Sometimes, the baby seems to make a connection that is so strong that it is almost as if the baby is desperately trying to "tell" mother something. For example, instances abound of pregnant women having to leave rock concerts because their babies refuse to calm down after being exposed to the high decibel noise levels. According to Dr. B.R.H. Van den Bergh of the University of Leuven in Belgium, this highlights both the sensitivity of the unborn child and another aspect of haptonomy. Dr. Janus concludes that "a huge, unusual human potential lies buried in this area of prenatal relating." (Veldman, F. 1994)

Subverted Truth

There are some possible summative guide-posts to watch for in communication and relationships. Communication is the primary vehicle to obtaining, maintaining, and sustaining good relationships. Therefore, adversity can reveal your personal personality, and that can translate into building character. Mistakes can be positive in that things are clarified, so now the relationship can have a positive sign, a passion for excellence, and a quest for maturation vs. negative signs, a passion for power, and less of a quest for stagnation.

Appreciation before Ambition

There is nothing wrong with making ambition a central focus of relationships. However, one may need to be appreciated before he or she achieves significant goals and desires because being ungrateful can expose itself by way of uncooperativeness. Being thankful for the other person can strengthen the relationship by making each person feel valued. Once this is established, the goals may be easier to achieve in the relationship.

When You Fall, Will Someone Catch You?

One of the highest, maybe *the* highest form of helping someone anytime, is to "advocate" for him or her. Being an advocate means doing whatever you can to support others, and if you support your mate, you build love and trust. The role of advocating is defined by the circumstances and situations that manifest themselves in problem-solving in relationships. If and when you fall or make a mistake, the other person must have insight on how to address your problem without unnecessarily "putting you down" or embarrassing you. After all, the advocacy role requires great insight into the other person's attitude and his or her reaction to situations.

Encircling Relationships with Communication

One quick thing you can do to improve your relationship with your significant other is to include a list of 3-5 questions or possible requests periodically for each other to answer. Questions and/or requests may include easy to understand and measurable ones that can or may be talked about. Also, seek various resources to answer the questions or requests, but at least give information that is applicable so that the communication skill-set gives positive direction to relationship-building.

Destruction of Anger and Bitterness

Both anger and bitterness are negative invaders that can destroy relationships. Anger is resentment with a history, and bitterness is a sharp, unpleasant, cynical feeling. Both interplay with each other to the extent that they take root in the mind and heart and take on a negative life of their own. This may harden the person to make quick decisions that inflict pain and possibly revenge on others. Then, the path or direction the relationship takes is defined as destructive.

Sometimes Effects Can Be More Powerful Than Positive Results

Many times, the results determine the success of relationships; thus, they are indeed important to recognize and act upon. But sometimes, the results may fall short as planned so that the effort should be equally recognized and put into action. This gives creditability to the relationship when the effort put into a relationship is included as a positive feature rather than always looking at the results. This way, positive efforts may not always equal positive results, but positive efforts keep the relationship afloat when you cannot see, feel, touch, taste, or smell the positive results. Thus, the effect becomes a genuine concern and desire for fostering good communication in relationships.

Dealing with Guilt

Guilt is usually a state of mind that occurs after an offense has happened. If not dealt with early on, it can expand to unhealthy regrets. For example, I know I have done something that's wrong, but for some reason I think the problem will dissipate over time. Now, I dismiss the problem; then, I deny and distort the problem to the extent that the same problem has become harder to solve because I didn't confront or deal with it when I should have. At this point the guilt can turn into blame, and the problems really start because the blame turns to shame; now, I am ashamed of being ashamed. To avoid this, one must confront or deal with problem situations in a timely manner when they arise. The three, guilt, blame and shame, usually unite for you to hold grudges against others involved in the relationship. A grudge is usually a state of mind that occurs after an offense has happened. If grudges are not dealt with early, they can lead to unhealthy regrets. Grudges can develop, grow, and mature like babies. Over time, the baby (grudge) is bred, carried, held, and nursed into existence. The trouble may be that anytime you cultivate and nurture something, it can become a part of your existence. Guilt is having feelings about the deeds you have committed. Blame is projecting these deeds onto others. Shame occurs when feelings are internalized. The reason that guilt, blame, and shame are so important is because the three usually work hand-in-hand to become toxic and debilitating in how we communicate in our relationships.

The Bystander Effect on Relationships

The presence of other people in your personal relationship tends to increase or decrease the ability to get help if needed. This is important because in private and public places people, more times than not, communicate differently. The bystander effect on relationships includes not so much what others may verbalize, but what they may not say or verbalize is also important. This may include a term known as the "eloquence of silence." Fathers, mothers, children, uncles, aunts, cousins and the entire family may need to learn how to stop talking so much. Usually, one can seldom be hurt by anything he or she did not say. The bystander method is utilized by being present for an advocacy or support role to your significant others in relationships. So the primary purpose is to allow verbalization to be abandoned at times to accommodate talkativeness in a non-verbal form, so that you can experience the quietness and stillness of your spirit on a daily basis. This allows you to listen actively and to assimilate thoughts of clarification. Sometimes, it is more valuable to remember that communication through silence may at times be more profitable in establishing and exhibiting self respect and value in others.

Transmitting Moods

Moods can be seen as social viruses with some people having a natural ability to transmit them to others. A mood is transmitted instantaneously and unconsciously within milliseconds, so quickly you can't control it and so subtle that you are unaware it has happened. Therefore, moods can be passed along from one person to another, but they are usually expressed at some inappropriate time and place. This is important because it's great to seek out a resource for support, but you should be discreet about using it. Some relationships invariably hurt worse because of this susceptibility to picking up someone else's mood. In general, you seek out people who have a similar mood as you because of your inability to maintain and integrate your sense of self.

The Test of Resolve in Relationships

Relationships survive when you are true to yourself, or to put it another way, when you "know thy self." When you are secure in who you are, you do not look to someone else to complete you. You are able to come to the table to share what you have to offer, instead of taking everything from the other person and looking for the other person to make you complete or happy. Fault- finding is the largest distraction in relationships because it again blames the other person for your own insecurities. This is indeed a test of resolve.

The Dynamics of Aircraft Flying as a Metaphor Relative to Communication and Relationships

It is interesting as well as mind-boggling to think of how a huge plane can fly through the air. There are four basic constructs that allow this to occur. Construct 1 is the "down" force, construct 2 is the "drag" force, construct 3 is the "thrust" force, and construct 4 is the "up" force. The "down" force is the weight of the aircraft, cargo, luggage, mail, passengers and even the paint on the aircraft. The "drag" force is the air friction and/or resistance of the airplane moving forward. The "thrust" force is the propelling of the engines that dictates the trajectory the airplane will take through the air. The "up" force is called the "lift" which keeps the aircraft in the air at the proper speed. Just as the dynamics are fundamentally in place for the aircraft to travel, so it is with communication and relationships. With these other factors playing a role for the aircraft to stay airborne, communication serves as the prime element that propels relationships through time. All relationships are challenged with flight turbulence, ups and downs, but the success of the relationship is predicated on how people communicate. Thus, the "thrust" would be the communication and the "up" force would be the relationship. So goes the thrust of the engines of communication; so goes the relationship through the perils of life.

Mindful Eating that May Determine Inter-Personal Results

Sometimes, what we do intra-personally (within) can impact others inter-personally (between). One thing to consider is mindful eating. Mindful eating by definition is when one develops a good relationship with his food, which can include appreciation, pleasure, and true satisfaction while eating. This sounds like simple jargon, but people don't learn how to utilize eating habits to potentially transform how they eat to improve their overall health and disengage from bad habits and behaviors. People are usually happy when they are eating. Babies exhibit and beam appreciation to the person that feeds them. They smile, move their arms, legs, and other areas to demonstrate their approval; so do adults. But many times we eat "on the go" and do not take the time to relax and truly enjoy our food. When we don't do this, we may miss out on the opportunity to think about the simple things in life that make us who we are, or an opportunity to spend quality time with our mates and/or children. Once we can achieve this, it gives us more self-control emotionally because we are doing something that is a natural phenomenon, eating, but with few or no restrictions. This can promote a sense of balance, choice, and acceptance of others, regardless of their failures. In other words, we continue to love the person although we dislike his or her behavior. One of the salient areas that can derive from mindful eating is the eloquence of silence. The primary purpose is to allow yourself to stop being verbal to accommodate the non-verbal. This way you can reach the stillness of the inner spirit that we experience daily but don't take advantage of. We learn to listen actively, assimilate thought of clarification, not justification, and respond to others admirably. Sometimes, it is more valuable to remember that communication through silence may say the most. Also, more times than not, silence helps you to understand yourself intra-personally and at the same time exhibit more respect for others, inter-personally. Much of this can be achieved by learning to utilize mindful eating to help facilitate communication in relationships.

Magnification vs. Minimization in Relationships

Firstly, magnification refers to looking at a negative experience and getting from that negative experience something positive. Secondly, magnification means looking at any experience, negative or positive, and reflecting with insight in order to gain more understanding in evaluating the experience. Looking at another person's flaws, shortcomings, and errors as though you don't have any shortcomings is magnification. Minimization refers to the tendency to criticize and underestimate the other person's good qualities. Now, the feelings and emotions are centralized to the point of being insensitive to the value and esteem of others. One of the greatest gifts in a relationship is to love others, accept them, forgive them, and reassure them. Magnification vs. minimization represents extreme levels of overestimation and underestimation of people, rather than accepting them as they are.

As one travels over the highways of relationships, one has to recognize signs for direction and places to stop for refreshing and re-servicing while on the trip. Knowing how to read the signs of life may determine the success of the trip. So it is with communication and relationships. Pit-stops and refueling along the way are a necessity.

There are studies, research articles, books, and magazines that examine communication in relationships in our contemporary world. From this massive list of works there are two major concepts that have become constant constructs in understanding communication in relationships. One is "pro-social behavior." Pro-social behavior occurs when someone acts to advocate, benefit, or support others without necessarily expecting any rewards to benefit themselves. The person performing the acts of kindness has no goal other than to help others. There are many people that are intrinsically motivated to help others out of the goodness of their heart. This is positive and deserves to be viewed as a tremendous avenue to both establish and maintain good communication with others. However, one has to be aware of people that will take advantage of others and their good deeds.

The other concept or construct is "passive aggressive behavior." Passive aggressive behavior is a condition in which a person actively complies with the idea of giving or receiving support to or from others, but resists the very act himself. So the person develops a personality of unexpressed anger and hostility. The problem is that the anger and hostility are internalized and the person interacts comfortably in the relationship, but in reality he or she is unhappy. A person with this behavior may appear to comply with another's wishes but sabotage the relationship because he or she has been taken for granted and manipulated. The internalized actions over time may exhibit anger that this individual has not expressed in words. Then, what can happen is one may become dependent in the relationship to the extent of trying to control others. The real downfall may be that the communication in the relationship becomes both ineffective and inefficient in the overall day-to-day interactions. Then everything becomes an issue:

Some Final Thoughts to Further Understand the Importance of Communication in Relationships

- Altered perceptions can make or break thought processes, but a violated conscience can shipwreck the mind.
- Anger is defined as resentment with a history. Some characteristics of anger are as follows:

  -Noise to the soul

  -Relentless invader of quietness

  -Invisible irritant of the mind and heart
- A passion for excellence brings about a quest for maturation.
- A passion for power brings about a quest for stagnation.
- Being ungrateful may translate to being uncooperative.
- "Big people" sometimes monopolize listening; "small people" sometimes monopolize talking.

- Celebrate someone else's accomplishments as if they are your own.
- Communication in relationships is enhanced when there is understanding and surrender, not when there is dominance and conquest.
- Communication in relationships evolves in three major ways: those who "ask" what happened; those who "make" things happen; and those who "watch" what happens.
- Deception and ignorance usually accompany each other.
- Devaluing others causes problems to be dismissed, denied, distorted and not dealt with.
- Developing a sense of powerlessness equates to rejection.
- Discouragement dulls desire; procrastination decreases opportunity.
- Don't exhaust all your feelings and surrender them to any earthly vessel.
- Don't use the comfort of the status quo as an excuse for not challenging stinking thinking.
- Encourage the discouraged.

- Failure to understand one's own past experiences can enable you to misunderstand future relationships.
- Find purpose in the mundane.
- Getting to the heart of a matter usually requires few words but great insight.
- Humility is not a weakness, but power under control and strength with direction.
- Jealousy and self-centeredness invite confusion.
- Know when to stop problem-focusing and start solution-focusing.
- Know when to take a seat; know when to take a stand.
- Know the difference between self-concept and self-esteem.
- Learn to doubt your doubts.
- Love's desire includes the value of respect.
- One doesn't have to accept or reject another's viewpoint; a point of neutrality may determine spontaneity and good decision-making.
- Optimism is the only legitimate attitude.

- Peace occurs when there is undisturbed composure of the mind.
- Peace provides calmness, encouragement, and healing.
- Problems are usually manifested by comparing, contrasting, justifying, all being irrationally disguised as rational.
- Putting feelings and emotions into words gives life to understanding differences of opinion.
- Remember the power and rewards of solitude.
- Self-fulfillment is not an individual goal; it is the consequence of life lived in service to others.
- Silence is not an adversary to avoid, but a close friend to embrace.
- Some things that can be debilitating in relationships are crowds, hurrying, and noise.
- The acceptance of a bad situation can be a resignation of the fact that you are more or less responsible.
- The continuance of justification is finding a viable solution to a problem, but saying that it is not the solution to the problem by using an excuse as to why the problem exists.

- The unfolding of problems is often more essential than finding solutions to them.
- Understand the presence of absence.
- Undisciplined feelings can become emotional lockdowns.
- Using thoughts, words, and actions helps to deter circumstances that intimidate, limit, or rule you.
- Utilize logic as a breakthrough for critical thinking.

This book is not all inclusive of information about good communication in relationships, but it teaches truths and helps equip you with some skill sets so that you can understand how to be balanced, knowledgeable, productive, and wise in how you communicate with others in your relationships.

Notes

Notes

Closing Remarks

With more than 35 years of experience as a global manager in a fortune 500 company, I encounter people and customers from many persuasions. Some of these relationships were established from business engagements, some from social activities, and others from personal contact. In hindsight, I could have been more effective had I understood the concepts Dr. Hall has skillfully interwoven in this book. Each nugget of wisdom establishes the foundation for helping many of the senior executives I coach on a regular basis. On a more personal note, I am grateful to Dr. Hall for sharing this useful information, and I will utilize it to further enhance my personal ability to motivate.

The challenge to establish and maintain healthy relationships requires thinking on several levels. Creating new mental models of how we interpret concepts in this book stands to improve our long term effectiveness. Making meaningful connections between communication, companionship, and character may become the most important thing you learn in life. Our ability to establish and maintain productive relationships will affect other success factors we aspire to achieve. Taking proactive steps over time leads to a complete transformation and improved outcomes. It all starts with an inward desire to learn and apply new knowledge as it is acquired.

The inability to connect relevant points is a problem many face when trying to implement personal changes. For example, it is difficult for a person to obtain constructive feedback when that person belittles a colleague in a public setting. Dr. Hall has put together powerful thoughts to help people "connect the dots." He has essentially given a road map for use to enhance your ability to understand basic components of communication in relationships. Its applicability is not relegated only to people with power and authority, but is for any person seeking improvement.

The stakes are high. I encounter people who struggle with this subject on a regular basis. Learning to work together does not necessarily come naturally. Nor is it always easy to implement the principles in this book. After years of work establishing and building healthy teams, I have learned that it takes thoughtful preparation and integration to help people understand how communication impacts relationships. The most impressive people I have ever experienced display an understanding of many of the concepts espoused in this publication.

Calvin Riley, CEO
Nehemiah The Leadership Company

References

Alexandra, Grace. (2004) *Emotional Bonding Too Close for Comfort,* Walden Publishing

Ballard, Joy. (2006). *Developmental Psychology* Class. A Student

Baron, Robert. A. (1996). *Essentials of Psychology.*

Bersheld E. & Peplan, L. A. (1983) *The Emerging Science of Relationships*

Brothers, Joyce. (2000) Parade Magazine, *Say "No to Happiness-Busters"*

Burney, Robert. (2005) *Dysfunctional Relationship Dynamics, Creative Mutilation* Canada Ltd.

Chambers, Reese. (2005) *Human Happiness: Its Nature and Its Attainment, Volume* II: Attachment of Happiness Chapter 16 Prentice Hall Publisher

Canary, Daniel. (2001) *Purpose of Relationships: What Is Healthy Behavior?* Elmhurst Publishing

Cormier, W. H. and Cormier, L. S. (1985) *Interview Strategies for Helpers: Fundamental Skills and Cognitive Behavioral Interventions*, 2nd Edition

DuBrin, Andrew J. (1997) *Human Relations: Interpersonal Job-oriented Skills*, Sixth Edition, Prentice Hall

Exley, Richard. (1993)*The Making of a Man*: *Devotions for The Challenges That Men Face In Family and Career*

Fisher, Terrance. (2002) *Biological Basis of Human Behavior: A Different Look at Human Behavior*. Elmhurst Publishing

Ford, Loren. (1996) *Game Plan*: *A Guide for Improving Human Relations and Personal Adjustment*

Halter, L.L. (1988) *Traits of Happy Couple,* Texas World Books Publisher

Harper, Gabe. (2005) *Relationship Soup Health Talk* Volume 9 Issues 3 McMaster Universities

Janus, Dr. Ludvig, (1997) The Enduring Effects of The Prenatal Experience, Northvale, New Jersey: Jason Aronson

Jean, Elsa. (1999) *Cognitive Dissonance Theory,* New York McGraw Hill Corupaniens, Inc.

Joyce, Carla. (2000) *Journal of Human Behavior in the Social Environment,* NY Rosen Publishing

Krumboltz, J. (1972) *Principles of Using Behavior Modification-Listening of Principles Adapted from Changing Children Behavior,* Prentice Hall

Kunssky, Judith. (2005) *The Guide to a Healthy Relationship,* Prentice Hall

Mayer, Richard J. (1990) *Conflict Management: The Courage To Confront,* Columbus Ohio: Batelle Press.

Oachs, Allie. (2005) *Loving Without Losing Yourself,* Wobart PTY LTD

Planalp, S., & Benson, A. (1992) *Friends and Acquaintances Conversations: Perceived Differences*

Prager, K.J. (1995) *The Psychology of Intimacy*

Reis, H. T. (1990) *The Role of Intimacy in Interpersonal Relations,* Journal of Social and Clinical Psychology, 9, 15-30

Sarafina, Edward P. (2001) *Behavior Modification,* 2nd edition Mayfield Publishing

Tannen, Deborah. (1996) *You Just Don't Understand: Women and Men in Conversation*, William Morrow and Company

Trait, Heather. (2001) *Recognizing Unhealthy Relationships,* Silence Speaks

Tucker, Joan. (2002) *Health Related Social Control within Older Adults Relationships,* Rand External Publication

The Geological Society of America

(1) Veldman, F. (1994) *Confirming Affectivity, The Dawn of Human Life and Prenatal,* Psychology and Medicine 6:1:11.26

(2) Juan, S. (1999) *Talking to the Unborn*, The Sun-Herald (Sydney)

Watkins, Kassie. (2006) Developmental Psychology, Class (A Student)

Wicks, R. J. (1979) *Helping Others: Ways of Listening, Sharing, and Counseling*, New York

Wright, H. Norman. (1987) *Understanding the Man in Your Life*, Waco: Word Book Publisher

Works Cited

Wikipedia.com

The PsiCafé http://www.psy.pdx.edu/PsiCafe/Areas/Developmental/AdultRelations/index.htm

The PsiCafé; http://www2.widener.edu/~dxr0006/proprium8.htm

Athabasca University;

http://psych.athabascau.ca/html/aupr/developmental.shtml

http://en.wikipedia.org/wiki/introversion

http://en.wikipedia.org/wiki/introversion#implications

http://www.learnhingplaceonline.com/relationships/friends/caringintrovert.htm

http://www.romanceopedia.com/I-Intimacydefined.html

Notes

Notes

Notes

Notes